Maths Spotlight

Activity Sheets

5

Heinemann

Series editors Peter Clarke
Len Frobisher

Writing team Janine Blinko
Paula Coombes
Hilary Koll
Steve Mills
Jeanette Mumford

Heinemann Educational Publishers
Halley Court, Jordan Hill, Oxford, OX2 8EJ
a division of Harcourt Education Ltd
www.heinemann.co.uk

Heinemann is a registered trademark of Harcourt Education Ltd

First published 2003

06 05 04 03
10, 9, 8, 7, 6, 5, 4, 3, 2, 1

ISBN 0 435 20726 1

Illustrated by Andy Hammond
Designed by Artistix
Cover illustration by Dave Cockburn
Cover design by Paul Goodman
Printed in the UK by Ashford Colour Press, Gosport, Hants

Contents

Numbers and the number system

Measures, shape and space

Handling data

Understanding place value

Activity Sheet 1

Name ....

Let's practise

1 What does the 7 in each number stand for?

a 54 **7**12 ____________ **b** 52 0**7**3 ____________

c 33**7** 334 ____________ **d** 3 50**7** 224 ____________

e 5 **7**53 009 ____________ **f** **7** 300 624 ____________

2 Write the total score each time.

a 3 50 000 10 400 ____________

b 600 70 1000 70 000 ____________

c 90 20 000 7000 500 6 800 000 ____________

d 400 1 000 000 30 000 9 20 200 000 ____________

3 Partition each number like the scores in question 2.

a 249 718 ________________________________

b 504 231 ________________________________

c 620 075 ________________________________

Let's solve problems

4 I'm thinking of a number between 3 299 875 and 3 300 015.
It is a multiple of 10, but not a multiple of 100. List the 12 possible numbers.

________ ________ ________ ________ ________ ________

________ ________ ________ ________ ________ ________

Let's investigate

5 Hawsker School is having a raffle.
The tickets are numbered 1 to 1000.
Investigate the number of tickets that have 1, 2 or 3 zeros.

? What if the tickets were numbered 1001 to 2000?

Rounding

Activity Sheet **2**

Name ....

Let's practise

1 Round each number to the **nearest 1000**.

a 7193 ____________ b 61 982 ____________

c 34 482 ____________ d 44 601 ____________ e 65 372 ____________

2 Approximate these totals by rounding to the **nearest 100**.

a 6145 + 3783 b 2843 + 3550 c 5902 + 6987

____________ ____________ ____________

____________ ____________ ____________

Now use a calculator to find the exact totals.

____________ ____________ ____________

3 Write three numbers that, when rounded to the nearest

a 10, give 54 250 ____________ ____________ ____________

b 100, give 31 200 ____________ ____________ ____________

c 1000, give 176 000 ____________ ____________ ____________

Let's solve problems

4 Write a situation and a number that you might round to the nearest

a 10 the number of children in my class, 27 → 30

b 100 ______________________________

c 1000 ______________________________

d 10 000 ______________________________

e 100 000 ______________________________

f 1 000 000 ______________________________

Positive and negative numbers (2)

Activity Sheet 3

Name ....

Let's practise

1 Continue each sequence with 3 more numbers.

a 35, 26, 17, 8, ____, ____, ____

b 44, 30, 16, 2, ____, ____, ____

c 48, 35, 22, 9, ____, ____, ____

d 38, 21, 4, ⁻13, ____, ____, ____

e ⁻51, ⁻39, ⁻27, ⁻15, ____, ____, ____

f ⁻71, ⁻55, ⁻39, ⁻23, ____, ____, ____

Let's play   A game for 2

- Draw 10 crosses on your grid at points where lines cross.
- Keep your grid secret.
- Take turns to say a pair of coordinates.
- A cross is zapped if its coordinates are said.
- Draw a ring round each zapped cross.
- The first to have all 10 crosses zapped is the loser.

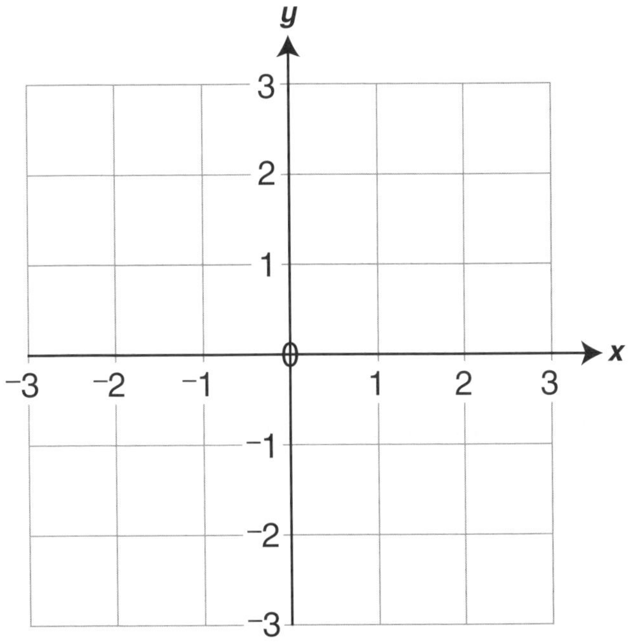

Let's investigate

2 Investigate all the pairs of integers on this number line that have a difference of 10.

________ ________ ________ ________ ________ ________

________ ________ ________ ________ ________

? What if the difference was 11, 12, ...?

Whole-number sequences (3)

Activity Sheet 4

Name ....

Let's practise

1 **a** This sequence starts at 0 and adds 4. Continue the sequence.

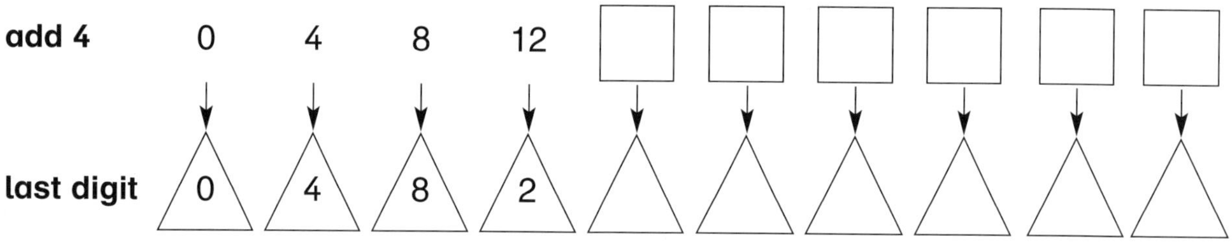

b Complete the last-digit pattern on the circle diagram.

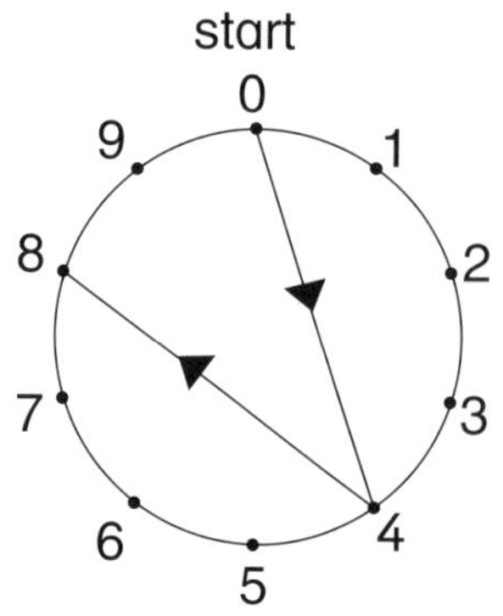

c Explain the pattern.

___

___

___

Let's investigate

2 **a** Investigate the last-digit patterns of these sequences.

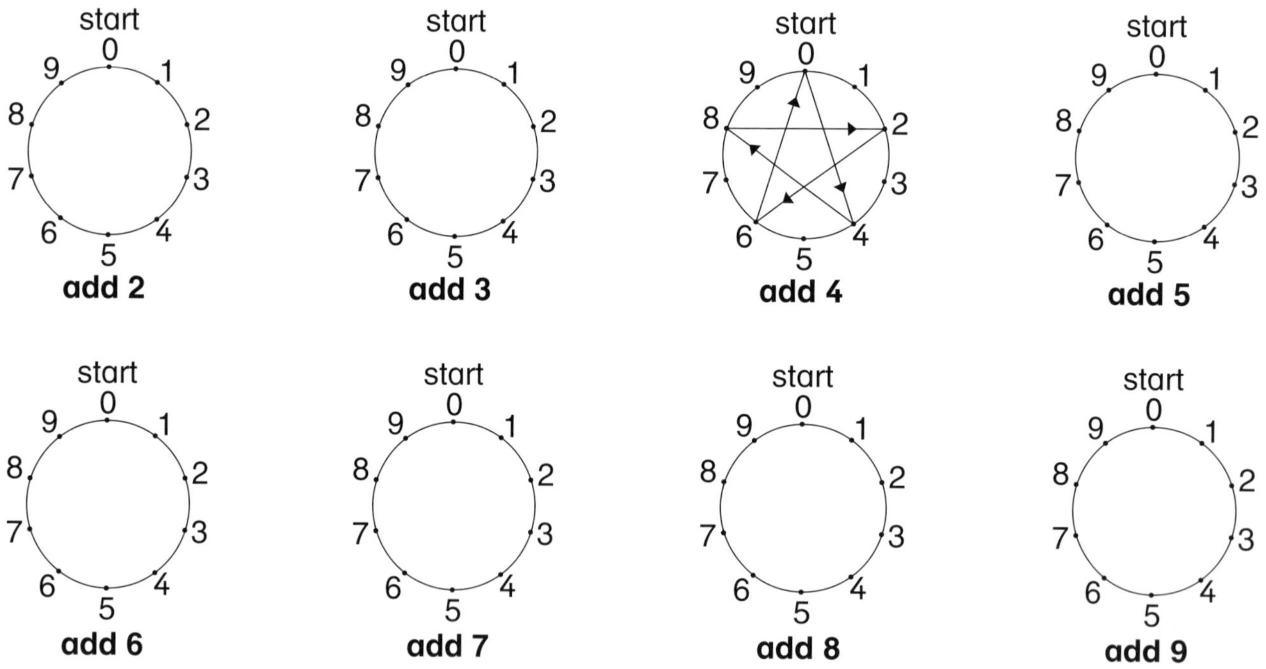

b Write about each pattern.

c In what ways are some of the patterns like each other?

Shape number patterns (1)

Activity Sheet 5

Name ....

Let's investigate

1 Each number in Pascal's triangle is made by adding the 2 numbers directly above it. Complete this part of Pascal's triangle.

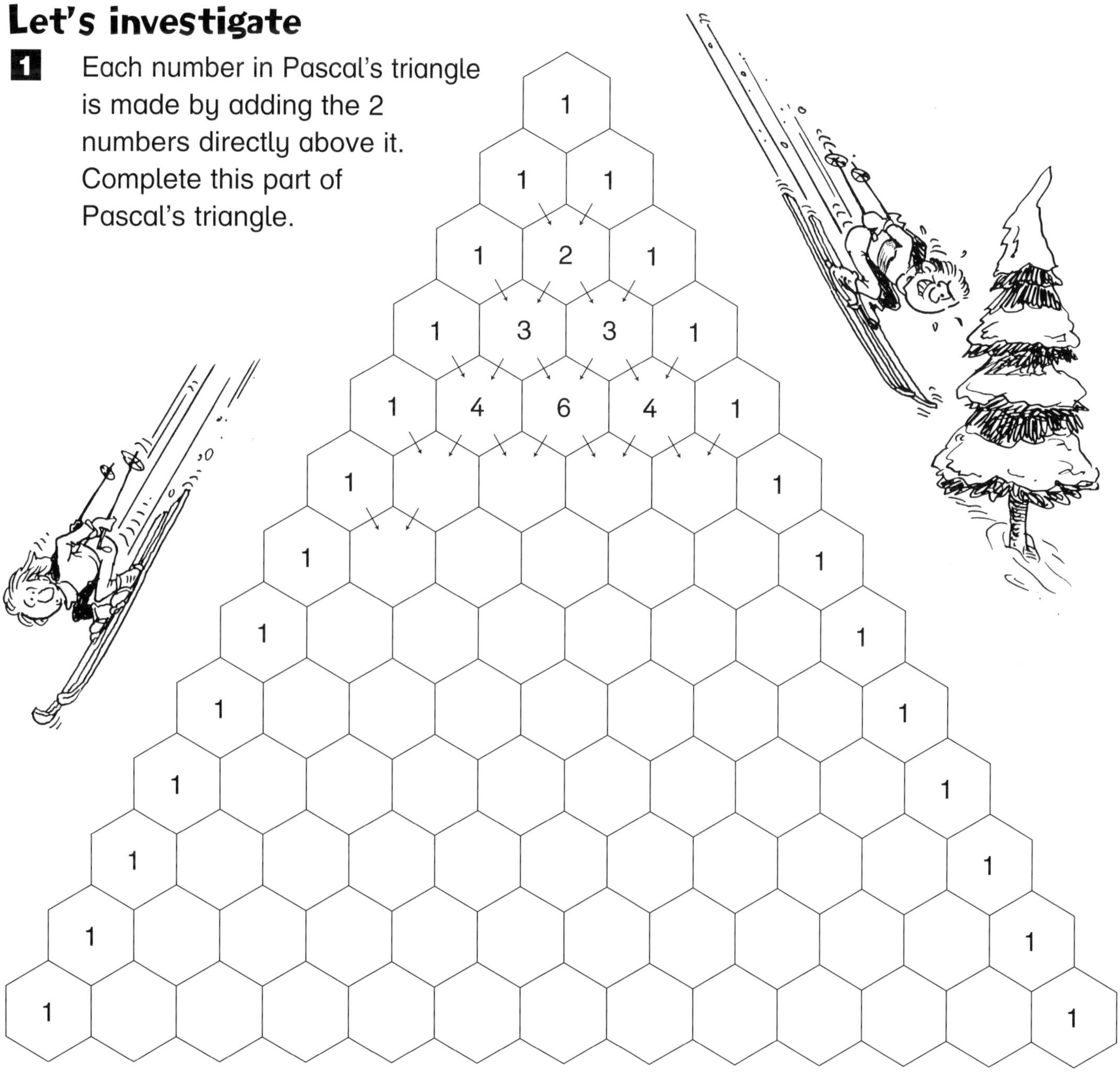

2 Write what you find out.

Look for patterns. Here are some ideas:

- patterns in the arrangement of odd or even numbers
- patterns in the arrangement of multiples of 3
- patterns in numbers that end in 0.

Look for other patterns.

? What if you take your Pascal's triangle and replace each number by the remainder when you divide that number by 5?

Shape number patterns (2)

Activity Sheet 6

Name ....

1 **a** Draw the next triangular number.

T(1) **T(2)** **T(3)** **T(4)** **T(5)**

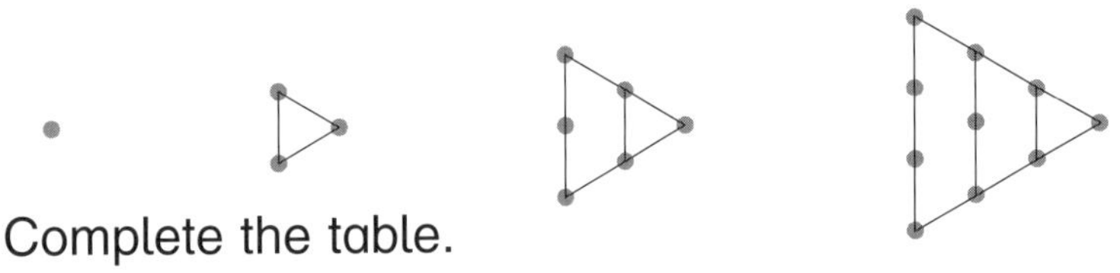

b Complete the table.

Triangle	T(1)	T(2)	T(3)	T(4)	T(5)	T(6)	T(7)	T(8)	T(9)	T(10)
Value	1	3	6							

2 Here are the first 5 pentagonal numbers.

P(1) **P(2)** **P(3)** **P(4)** **P(5)**

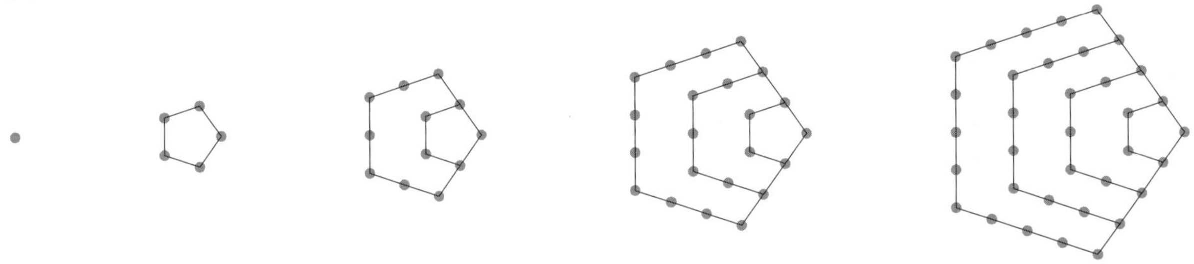

Complete the table for P(3), P(4) and P(5).
Find a pattern to help you complete the rest of the values.

Pentagon	P(1)	P(2)	P(3)	P(4)	P(5)	P(6)	P(7)	P(8)	P(9)	P(10)
Value	1	5								

Let's investigate

3 Complete the table for the triangular and pentagonal numbers.
Investigate what the square and hexagonal numbers are.

Number / **Polygon**	**1**	**2**	**3**	**4**	**5**	**6**	**7**	**8**	**9**	**10**
Triangle	1	3								
Square	1	4								
Pentagon	1	5								
Hexagon	1	6								

Investigating odd and even numbers

Activity Sheet 7

Name ....

Let's practise

1 Complete using different even numbers (E).

(E) × (E) = ( )
8 × 4 = [ ]

(E) × (E) = ( )
[ ] × [ ] = [ ]

(E) × (E) = ( )
[ ] × [ ] = [ ]

(E) × (E) = ( )
[ ] × [ ] = [ ]

2 Complete each statement and write 2 examples that satisfy it.

a The product of 2 odd numbers is an ______ number.

[ ] × [ ] = [ ] [ ] × [ ] = [ ]

b The product of an odd and an even number is an ______ number.

[ ] × [ ] = [ ] [ ] × [ ] = [ ]

c Double an odd number plus 1 is an ______ number.

double [ ] + 1 = [ ] double [ ] + 1 = [ ]

d 3 times an even number minus 1 is an ______ number.

3 × [ ] − 1 = [ ] 3 × [ ] − 1 = [ ]

Let's investigate

3 Investigate Sarah's statement.

? What if 'add 1 to' was 'subtract 1 from'?

Looking at divisibility (1)

Activity Sheet 8

Name ....

You need

coloured pencils

Let's practise

1 Colour a quarter of each box if its number is divisible by:

3 → red **5 → green**
7 → blue **11 → yellow.**

101	102	103	104	105	106	107	108	109	110
111	112	113	114	115	116	117	118	119	120
121	122	123	124	125	126	127	128	129	130
131	132	133	134	135	136	137	138	139	140
141	142	143	144	145	146	147	148	149	150
151	152	153	154	155	156	157	158	159	160
161	162	163	164	165	166	167	168	169	170
171	172	173	174	175	176	177	178	179	180
181	182	183	184	185	186	187	188	189	190
191	192	193	194	195	196	197	198	199	200

a List the numbers that are divisible by 3 and 5.

____

b List the numbers that are divisible by 5 and 7.

____

c List the numbers that are divisible by 3, 5 and 11.

____

d Explain why there are no numbers with 4 colours.

____

2 Complete the table by writing each missing ✓ and ✗.

	÷ 3	÷ 4	÷ 5	÷ 6	÷ 8	÷ 9	÷ 10	÷ 25
135	✓	✗	✓	✗	✗	✓	✗	✗
273								
300								
a	✓	✓	✗	✓	✗	✗	✗	✗

Suggest 3 different numbers that could go in box **a**. ________ ________ ________

Let's investigate

3 Investigate the sets of numbers that are divisible by 3, 4, 5, 6, 8, 9 or 10.
Try and find patterns to help you make a rule that relates each factor to its set of numbers.

? What if you investigated sets of numbers that are **not** divisible by 3, 4, 5, 6, 8, 9 or 10?

Common multiples of 2 or 3 numbers

Activity Sheet 9

Name ....

Let's practise

1 Tick the numbers that are multiples of 7.
Put a cross through the numbers that are multiples of 2.

917 2898 747 1206

1106 3808 921 749

Let's play A game for 2

You need
scissors

- Cut out the number cards below.
- Decide who is 'odd' and who is 'even'.
- Each choose any 2 of the numbers and calculate their lowest common multiple (LCM).
- Record the numbers and LCMs in the table.
- Work out the difference between the two LCMs.
- If the difference is odd then 'odd' scores a point; if it is even then 'even' scores a point.
- The winner is the player with more points after 7 games.

Odd		Even		Difference between LCMs
Name:		Name:		
Numbers	LCM	Numbers	LCM	

What if each player chose 3 numbers?

2	3	4	5	6	7	8
9	10	11	12	13	14	15
16	17	18	19	20	21	22

Using square numbers

Activity Sheet 10

Name ....

Let's practise

1 **a**

	10^2	15^2	20^2	25^2	30^2	35^2	40^2
	100	225					

difference	125					
difference	50					

b Without your calculator, use the diagram above to work out the value of these square numbers.

$45^2 =$ ☐ $50^2 =$ ☐ $55^2 =$ ☐

2 Use the value of the square numbers in question 1 to help you work out these multiplications without a calculator. Show your working.

a $16 \times 15 =$	**b** $21 \times 20 =$	**c** $26 \times 25 =$	**d** $49 \times 50 =$

Let's investigate

3 **a** Continue this sequence of triangular numbers.

1 3 6 10 15 ☐ ☐ ☐ ☐ ☐ ☐

b Investigate the sums of pairs of triangular numbers. Record in the table.

Triangular number	1									
Triangular number	3									
Sum	4									

c Which pairs of triangular numbers have a sum that is a square number?

Looking for patterns

Activity Sheet 11

Name ....

Let's practise

1 Write the answers.

$1 \times 1 =$ ______	$11 \times 1 =$ ______
$11 \times 11 =$ ______	$11 \times 11 =$ ______
$111 \times 111 =$ ______	$11 \times 111 =$ ______
$1111 \times 1111 =$ ______	$11 \times 1111 =$ ______
$11\,111 \times 11\,111 =$ ______	$11 \times 11\,111 =$ ______

Let's investigate

2 **a** Calculate the answer to each multiplication.

$3 \times 3 =$ ______	$4 \times 9 =$ ______
$3 \times 33 =$ ______	$44 \times 9 =$ ______
______ = ______	______ = ______
______ = ______	______ = ______
______ = ______	______ = ______
______ = ______	______ = ______

b Write 2 more multiplications in each pattern. Find the answers.

c Investigate patterns in the answers.

d Predict the next 2 lines in each pattern.

e Use a calculator to check your predictions.

? What if you started with other sets of numbers?

Changing and reducing fractions

Activity Sheet 12

Name ....

Let's practise

1

a $\frac{5}{40} = \frac{\square}{8}$ b $\frac{2}{100} = \frac{1}{\square}$ c $\frac{\square}{30} = \frac{\square}{5}$

d $\frac{9}{\square} = \frac{\square}{20}$ e $\frac{8}{\square} = \frac{1}{5}$ f $\frac{\square}{100} = \frac{4}{\square}$

2

a $\frac{40}{7} = \square\frac{5}{7}$ b $\frac{\square}{3} = 6\frac{2}{\square}$ c $\frac{50}{6} = 8\frac{\square}{3}$

d $\frac{\square}{10} = 2\frac{1}{2}$ e $\frac{\square}{8} = 7\frac{1}{2}$ f $\frac{\square}{10} = \square\frac{2}{5}$

Let's play A game for 2

- Each shuffle both your packs of cards separately.
- Put your packs face down in two piles, the 1–10 digit cards above the multiples-of-10 cards.
- Take turns to turn over the top card from each pile. Put it face up alongside the pile.
- Record the fraction and reduce it if possible.
- Score 1 point for each equivalent fraction.
- Continue until all cards have been used and total your points.
- The winner is the player with more points.

You each need

1–10 digit cards, all multiples-of-10 cards from 10 to 100

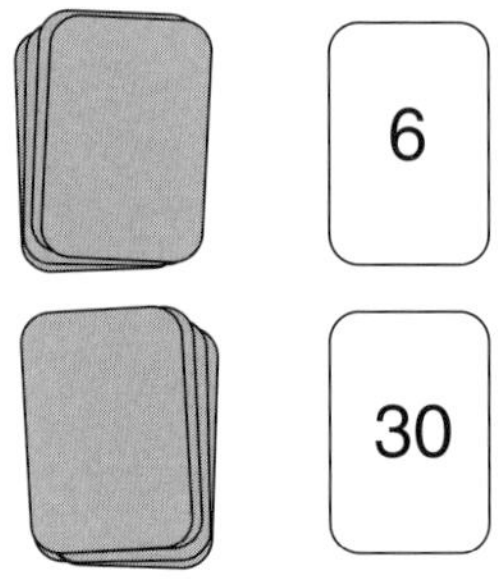

$\frac{6}{30} = \frac{3}{15} = \frac{1}{5}$

Scores 3 points.

? What if you placed the multiples-of-10 cards above the 1–10 digit cards and made mixed numbers?

Ordering fractions (2)

Activity Sheet 13

Name ....

Let's play
A game for 2

You need
4 dice

- Take turns to roll the 4 dice. If any dice shows 5, roll it again until you have 4 numbers that are not 5.
- Record the 4 numbers as 2 proper fractions.
- Write the 2 fractions on a number line below.
- Score points equal to a number of twelfths that lie between the 2 fractions on the line.
- Try to choose fractions that have the fewest twelfths between them.
- The loser is the player who reaches 20 points first.

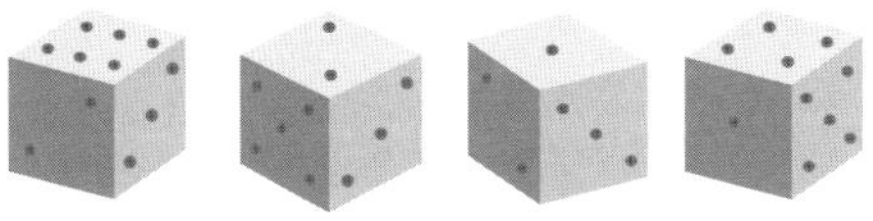

I can make $\frac{2}{6}$ and $\frac{1}{4}$, $\frac{1}{2}$ and $\frac{4}{6}$ or $\frac{2}{4}$ and $\frac{1}{6}$.

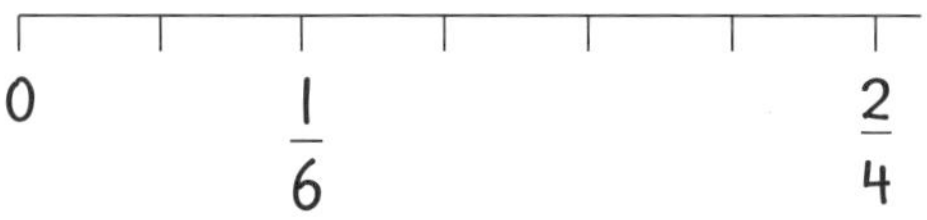

$\frac{1}{6}$ and $\frac{2}{4}$ have $\frac{3}{12}$, $\frac{4}{12}$ and $\frac{5}{12}$ between them.

Score 3 points.

Fractions and division (2)

Activity Sheet 14

Name ....

Let's practise

1

a $2\frac{1}{2} = \frac{\square}{2}$ b $6\frac{1}{2} = \frac{\square}{2}$ c $3\frac{1}{\square} = \frac{7}{\square}$

d $1\frac{1}{4} = \frac{\square}{4}$ e $4\frac{\square}{4} = \frac{19}{4}$ f $3\frac{1}{8} = \frac{\square}{8}$

g $7\frac{1}{\square} = \frac{\square}{4}$ h $5\frac{1}{\square} = \frac{44}{8}$ i $6\frac{\square}{\square} = \frac{50}{8}$

2

a $\frac{3}{5}$ of £1 = $\square$ p b $\frac{5}{8}$ of 48 m = $\square$ m c $\frac{7}{\square}$ of 112 = 98

d $\frac{4}{\square}$ of 490 = 280 e $\frac{\square}{10}$ of 200 = 140 f $\frac{5}{\square}$ of 1 hr = $\square$ min

Let's play A game for 2

You need
counters in 2 colours

- Take turns to choose a number and a fraction.
- Find the fraction of the number.
  If your answer is in the grid, cover it with a counter.
- You can use the numbers and fractions as often as you like.
- The winner is the first player with 4 counters in a row in any direction.

Numbers

15 400

24 16 200

30 56

Fractions

$\frac{3}{8}$ $\frac{7}{10}$

$\frac{2}{3}$ $\frac{4}{5}$ $\frac{9}{100}$

$\frac{3}{4}$ $\frac{5}{6}$

6	42	16	24
36	90	320	10
20	300	25	140
280	12	80	21

Ratio and proportion (2)

Activity Sheet 15

Name ....

You need
coloured pencils

Let's practise

1 Colour each pattern using yellow and blue so that:

a the ratio is 3 blue squares to every 1 yellow square

b the proportion of yellow squares is $\frac{1}{3}$ of the row.

Let's solve problems

2 Choose 2 different coloured shapes to design a pattern on the grid. In your pattern:

- the sizes of the 2 coloured shapes must be in the ratio of 2 to 1.
- the proportion of the grid covered by all the shapes must be $\frac{2}{3}$.

Using decimals (2)

Activity Sheet 16

Name ....

Let's practise

3 6 7 6

1 Use these 4 digits to make 12 different numbers, each with a units digit and 3 decimal places. Write them in order, starting with the largest.

□·□□□ □·□□□ □·□□□ □·□□□

□·□□□ □·□□□ □·□□□ □·□□□

□·□□□ □·□□□ □·□□□ □·□□□

Which of these decimal numbers lies between 3·66 and 3·67? ____________

Write 3 more decimal numbers that lie between 3·66 and 3·67. ____________

Let's play A game for 2

You need
4 dice

- Roll the 4 dice. Use the 4 digits to make a target number with a units digit and 3 decimal places.
- Each roll the 4 dice and use your digits to make a decimal number as near as possible to the target number. Record it in the table.
- Score 1 point if your number is nearer to the target.
- Repeat for 4 more target numbers.
- The winner is the player with more points. Play again.

Target number 1·146

	Target number	Name: Number	Name: Number	Point awarded to
1	□·□□□			
2				
3				
4				
5				

Using decimals (3)

Activity Sheet 17

Name ....

Let's play

A game for 2

This is a mastermind game of strategy.

Find the secret number in 10 or fewer guesses to win.

- Player 1 chooses and records a number secretly. It must have a units digit, 3 decimal places and no repeated digits.
- Player 2 has a guess at the number and writes it down in the first table below.
- Player 1 gives 1 point for each correct digit and 1 point for each correct place.
- Player 2 keeps guessing, using the information, until they find the secret number or have used 10 guesses.
- Now swap so Player 2 chooses a secret number.
- Who finds the secret number more quickly?

The secret number is 1·456.

Game 1		
Guess U · t h th	Points for	
	Digits correct	Places correct
1 · 2 3 4	2	1
5 · 6 7 8	2	0
1 · 5 6 7	3	1

Game 1		
Guess U · t h th	Points for	
	Digits correct	Places correct

Game 2		
Guess U · t h th	Points for	
	Digits correct	Places correct

Fractions and equivalent decimals (2)

Activity Sheet **18**

Let's play

A game for 2

You need

scissors

- Cut out the fraction cards below.
- Shuffle them and place them face down in a pile.
- Player 1 takes two cards from the top of the pile.
- They decide which fraction is bigger and place it face up next to the pile.

Player 1 may not use anything to help them. They cannot change their mind once they have put the card down!

- Player 2 uses the calculator to check by turning both fractions into decimal fractions.
- Player 1 scores 1 point for every correct decision.
- Repeat until all the cards are used. Then swap roles.
- After 2 rounds, the player with more points wins.

$\frac{7}{20}$	$\frac{3}{10}$	$\frac{6}{100}$	$\frac{3}{15}$	$\frac{1}{2}$
$\frac{13}{40}$	$\frac{305}{1000}$	$\frac{8}{25}$	$\frac{3}{4}$	$\frac{5}{8}$
$\frac{1}{5}$	$\frac{16}{30}$	$\frac{99}{1000}$	$\frac{4}{9}$	$\frac{3}{5}$
$\frac{25}{1000}$	$\frac{45}{50}$	$\frac{1}{8}$	$\frac{1}{3}$	$\frac{5}{6}$

Fractions and equivalent percentages

Let's play A game for 2

You need
scissors

- Cut out the fraction and percentage cards below.
- Shuffle the fractions and percentages separately and place them face down in 2 piles.
- Player 1 takes one card from the top of each pile.
- If they think the cards are equivalent, they put them together face up. If not, they put them face down.

Player 1 may not use anything to help them. They cannot change their mind once they have put the cards down!

- Player 2 uses the calculator to check by turning both fractions into decimal fractions and then percentages.
- Player 1 scores 1 point for every correct decision.
- Repeat until all the cards are used. Then swap roles.
- After 2 rounds, the player with more points wins.

$\frac{7}{20}$	$\frac{3}{10}$	$\frac{6}{100}$	$\frac{3}{5}$	$\frac{1}{2}$
$\frac{1}{3}$	$\frac{1}{4}$	$\frac{8}{25}$	$\frac{3}{4}$	$\frac{45}{50}$
25%	35%	90%	50%	32%
6%	$33\frac{1}{3}\%$	60%	30%	75%

Finding percentages

Name ....

Let's practise

1

a $30\% = \frac{□}{10}$

b $80\% = \frac{4}{□}$

c $□\% = \frac{3}{4}$

d $40\% = \frac{□}{5}$

e $25\% = \frac{1}{□}$

f $10\% = \frac{□}{10}$

g $□\% = \frac{3}{□}$

h $□\% = \frac{□}{20}$

i $□\% = \frac{□}{□}$

2

a 15% of £1 = □ p

b 36% of 1 km = □ m

c 73% of 1 kg = □ g

d □ % of 84 = 21

e 20% of □ = 40

f 75% of □ = □

Let's play A game for 2

- Take turns to choose a number and a percentage.
- Find the percentage of the number.
  If your answer is in the grid, cover it with a counter.
- You can use the numbers and percentages as often as you like.
- The winner is the first player with 4 counters in a row in any direction.

You need
counters in 2 colours

Numbers

400 24

130 16 200

30 56

Percentages

30% 70%

25% 80% 9%

75% 40%

6	120	160	18
36	9	320	42
14	100	24	104
280	12	52	21

Recall of addition and subtraction facts

Activity Sheet **21**

Name ....

Let's practise

1 Subtract each of the numbers in the first grid from 100 as quickly as you can. Write the answers in the second grid. Check each of your answers by adding.

32	78	54	77	86	98
49	64	38	43	61	87
73	52	18	27	63	83

68					

2 Put a ring around each pair that has a total of 1 or 10.

2·5 6·5   8·7 2·3   0·9 0·1   0·7 0·4   6·7 4·3   1·1 8·9

8·2 1·8   3·8 6·2   4·8 5·2   7·4 2·6   1·2 9·8   0·6 0·4

Write the totals of those pairs that are *not* 1 or 10. ______________________

3 To win a prize a person must score 1000 points.
Write how many more points each person needs.

750 _____   350 _____   800 _____   850 _____   600 _____   95 _____

Let's investigate

4 Follow the instructions below.
Write all the results in one column of the table.

- Pick a whole number between 1 and 50.
- Subtract this number from 100.
- Divide the answer by 10.
- Subtract this number from 10.
- Multiply the answer by 100.
- Subtract this number from 1000.
- Divide the answer by 10.
- Subtract this number from 100.

Use the same instructions to fill in the other columns.

47							
53							
5·3							
4·7							
470							
530							
53							
47							

Write about any relationship you notice between the start and end numbers. Explain why.

Addition and subtraction

Activity Sheet **22**

Name ....

Let's practise

1 Use this subtraction fact to help answer each question: 9857 – 5873 = 3984

a 9857 – 3984 = ______

b 3984 + 5873 = ______

c 9857 – ______ = 5873

d 5873 + ______ = 9857

e ______ + 5873 = 9857

f ______ – 5873 = 3984

2 Use 3 of these runners' numbers each time to make as many different addition and subtraction statements as you can.

Additions	Subtractions
2119 + 2406 = 4525	4525 – 2406 = 2119

Let's solve problems

3 a If I subtract it from 3850 I get a number that is 2835 greater than 180.

What is my number? __________

b If I subtract it from 8695 I get a number that is 146 greater than 3462.

What is my number? __________

c If I subtract it from 4843 I get a number that is 437 less than 1980.

What is my number? __________

d If I subtract it from 4972 I get a number that is 3073 less than 5936.

What is my number? __________

Written addition (3)

Activity Sheet **23**

Name ....

Let's practise

1 Write in the missing digits.

a

	7	□	4	8
+	6	2	8	□
1	3	6	3	2

b

	4	□	3	7
+	5	8	6	□
1	□	3	0	4

c

	6	4	□	9
+	2	□	5	□
	□	3	4	2

Check your answers.

Let's solve problems

2 A van can carry a maximum of 1000 kg.

a What is the greatest number of boxes that can be loaded on the van? ____________

b What is the total mass of the boxes in the van? ____________

c What is the total mass of any boxes that are left? ____________

Let's investigate

3 Use the digits 6 7 8 9 to write as many 4-digit numbers as possible.

Investigate the sums of pairs of your numbers.

Write one sum in each section of the sorting box.

Answer is between						
13 000 and 14 000	**14 000 and 15 000**	**15 000 and 16 000**	**16 000 and 17 000**	**17 000 and 18 000**	**18 000 and 19 000**	**19 000 and 20 000**
			8967 + 7698 = 16665			

Written subtraction (2)

Activity Sheet 24

Name ....

You need
coloured pencils

Let's solve problems

1

a Last year a football stadium had 8593 seats. This year, some building work increased the number of seats to 9312. How many new seats were added?

b At last week's match there were 4897 more people than at this week's match. Last week there were 7124 people. How many were there this week?

c There were 9815 people at a match, including adults and children. If 846 were children and 3871 were women, how many were men?

d A stadium has 4729 seats. 195 seats are empty and 678 are taken by children. How many seats are taken by adults?

e If 3725 more seats are taken by adults than by children, and 5032 seats are taken by adults, how many are taken by adults and children together?

f At this week's match there were 3375 more people than at last week's match. If there had been 128 more this week, there would have been 9999 people. How many were there last week?

Colour the answers in the grids. What 3-letter word can you see?

4370	3076
2604	5098
5920	6790

1790	5602	4156
1281	719	3777
4246	2277	1307

3773	2504	1137
6339	6504	2227
3856	4246	6496

Let's investigate

2

- Choose 4 digits from 1 to 9.
- Use them to write a 4-digit number, such as 4738.
- Reverse the digits to make another number.
- Find the difference between these 2 numbers.
- Keep on doing this until you come to an 'ending'.
- Write about the different 'endings' and patterns in the numbers.

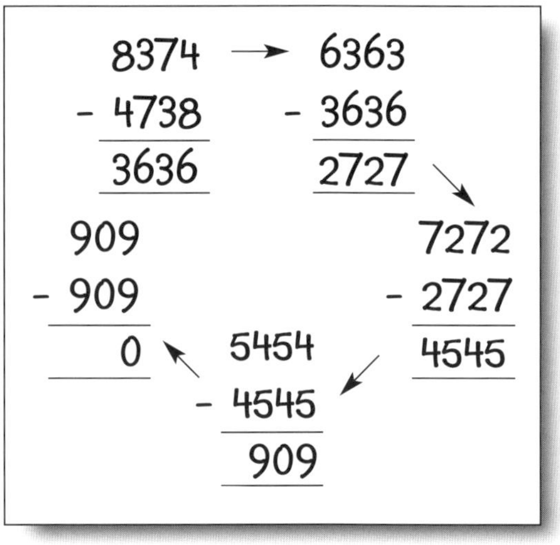

Checking addition and subtraction

Activity Sheet 25

Name ....

Let's practise

1 Tick the answer in each oval that you think could be the answer.

a

```
   2 _ _ 8
 + 6 _ 8 3
 ---------
```

b

```
   7 _ _ 7
 − 5 _ 6 5
 ---------
```

c

```
   6 4 _ 2
 − 5 _ 6 8
 ---------
```

a: **9301**, **8840**, **8681**, **10 471**

b: **2348**, **2502**, **1042**, **1123**

c: **1036**, **334**, **834**, **1004**

Let's solve problems

2 The judge of the water-skiing contest is holding up a set of three 4-digit numbers.

The total of the 3 cards is 3340.

The difference between any 2 of my cards is never greater than 5.

All 3 numbers are multiples of 5.

When I find the differences between different pairs of my cards I can get an even number or an odd number.

The total of the 3 cards is 19 985.

The difference between any 2 of my cards is never greater than 5.

All 3 numbers are multiples of 5.

When I find the differences between different pairs of my cards I can get an even number or an odd number.

What are the numbers on the cards?

a ☐ ☐ ☐   **b** ☐ ☐ ☐

Solving percentage problems

Activity Sheet 26

Name ....

Let's practise

1 Complete the diagrams.

a

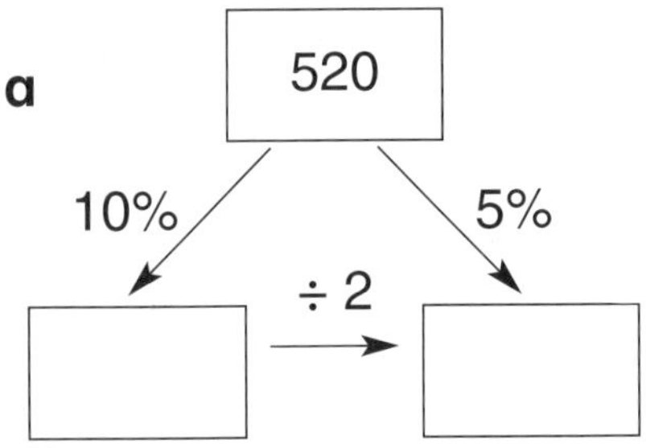

b

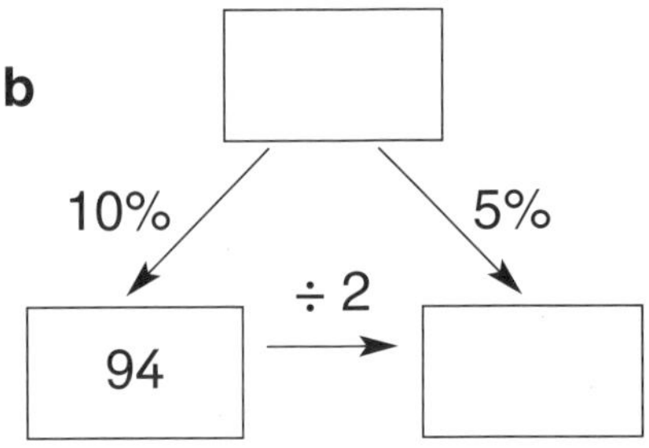

c

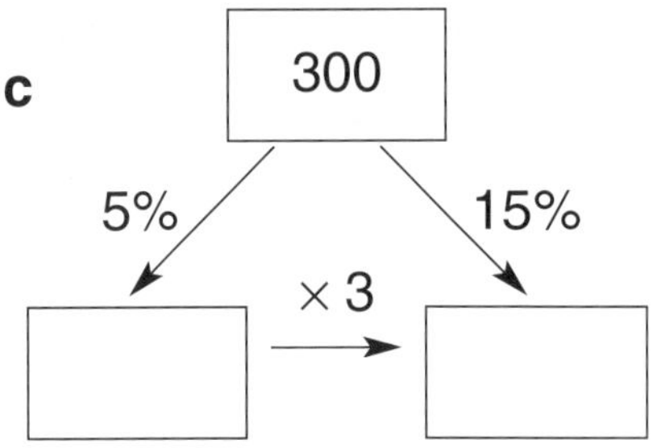

Let's solve problems

2 Jamie puts money into a bank account. Each year he saves 10% more money. Complete this table.

Year	Amount	10%	New amount
1999	£1000	£100	£1100
2000	£1100		
2001			
2002			
2003			

Total added:	

3 An estate agent charges a 5% fee for selling a house.

You need
coloured pencils

£98 000 **£275 000** **£130 000** **£49 000** **£4 000 000**

a If the fee was between £2500 and £5000, which house did he sell? Colour it yellow.

b If the fee was between £9000 and £15 000, which house did he sell? Colour it red.

c If the fee was between £5000 and £7500, which house did he sell? Colour it blue.

Division and fractions

Activity Sheet 27

Name ....

Let's solve problems

1 Grain is shared equally between traders.
Complete the table to show how much each trader gets as a mixed number of kilograms.

	4 traders each have:	5 traders each have:	6 traders each have:	7 traders each have:
67 kg of grain	$16\frac{3}{4}$ kg	$13\frac{2}{5}$ kg		
37 kg of grain	$9\frac{1}{4}$ kg			
49 kg of grain				
90 kg of grain				

Let's play

A game for 2

You need
2 dice, a different coloured pencil each

Each player:

- Chooses a number from the grid.
- Divides their grid number by 7.
- Records the answer as a mixed number.
  Example: $69 \div 7 = 9\frac{6}{7}$
- Rolls the 2 dice.
- Colours the grid number if the number on either dice equals the numerator in the mixed number.
  Example:  and $9\frac{6}{7}$, so 69 is coloured.

The first to colour 5 numbers is the winner.

81	53	116	97	96	101
123	99	88	73	111	79
114	90	76	87	69	103
110	115	100	78	113	117

Let's investigate

2 The numbers in all the triangles are different and they are all between 100 and 150.
Investigate what the numbers could be. Complete each division.

△ $\div 8 =$ ☐ $\frac{5}{8}$ △ $\div 8 =$ ☐ $\frac{5}{8}$ △ $\div 8 =$ ☐ $\frac{5}{8}$

△ $\div 8 =$ ☐ $\frac{5}{8}$ △ $\div 8 =$ ☐ $\frac{5}{8}$ △ $\div 8 =$ ☐ $\frac{5}{8}$

? What if the incomplete division was △ $\div 8 =$ ☐ $\frac{7}{8}$?

Division facts

Activity Sheet **28**

Name ....

Let's practise

1 **a** One sixth of 54 is ____ **b** 56 shared between 7 is ____

c 64 divided by ____ is 8 **d** There are ____ nines in 72

e ____ divided by 6 is 7 **f** ____ ________ of 36 is 27

2 Complete the table, dividing each number on the left by each number in the top row.

You need
coloured pencils

- If the numbers divide exactly, write the quotient in the square.
- If the numbers do not divide exactly, colour the square.

	divided by								
	2	**3**	**4**	**5**	**6**	**7**	**8**	**9**	**10**
36	18								
40									
54									
63									
72									
83									

Let's play A game for 2

You need
2 dice, a set of 2–10 number cards

- Each player is dealt 4 number cards.
- Player 1 rolls both dice to make a 2-digit number.

Example:  and  can be 24 or 42.

- Player 2 then rolls the dice and chooses a number.
- One point is scored for each number card that divides exactly into the 2-digit number.
- The first to reach 10 points is the winner.

Doubling, halving and squaring

Name ....

Let's practise

1
a Double 47 is ____
b Half of 158 is ____
c Twice ____ is 178
d Half of ______ is 1120
e ______ divided by 2 is 1450
f ____ times 970 is 1940

2 Each board has a square of dots. Some of the dots are hidden.
How many dots are in each square?

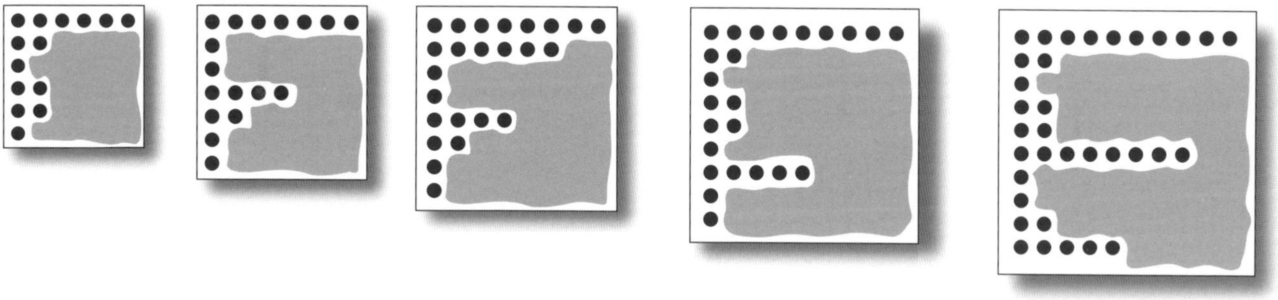

a ______ b ______ c ______ d ______ e ______

3 How many dots would there be in a

a 20×20 square ______
b 30×30 square ______
c 40×40 square ______
d 50×50 square ______
e 60×60 square ______
f 70×70 square ______
g 80×80 square ______
h 90×90 square? ______

Let's investigate

4 Investigate the squares of 1, 11, 111, …

1^2 = ________ 11^2 = ________ 111^2 = ________

1111^2 = ____________ $11\,111^2$ = ____________

What do you notice?
Predict further squares in the pattern.
Write about any patterns you notice.

? What if you investigated 1^2, 101^2, 1001^2, $10\,001^2$, …?

Using factors

Activity Sheet 30

Name ....

Let's practise

1 Use factors to complete each diagram.

a

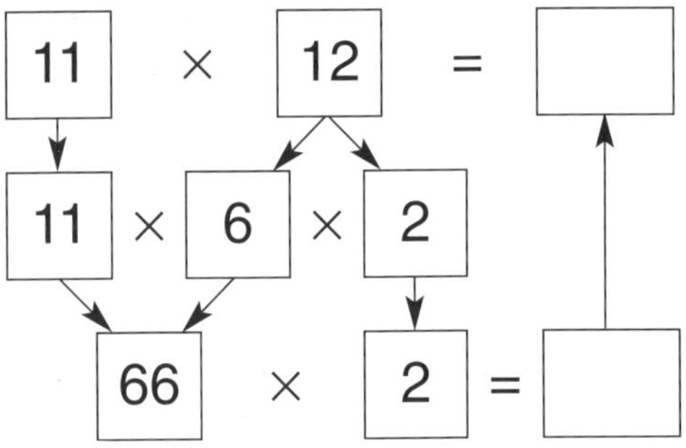

b

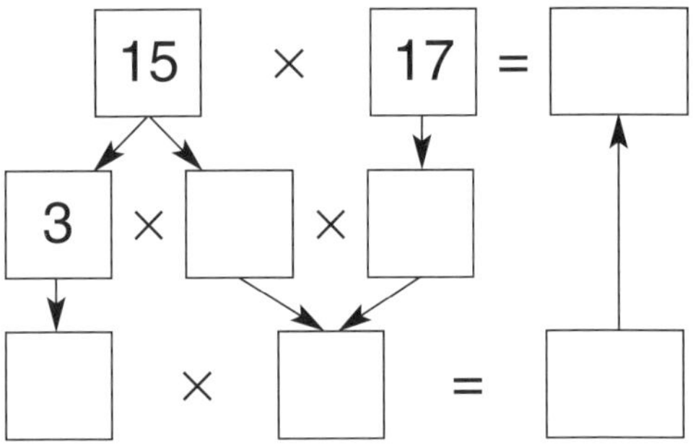

2 Use factors to complete each multiplication.

a $15 \times 32 = 3 \times 5 \times 32$

$= 3 \times$ ______

$=$ ______

b $24 \times 14 = 24 \times 7 \times$ ______

$=$ ______ $\times$ ______

$=$ ______

c $28 \times 21 =$ ______ $\times 7 \times 3$

$=$ ______ $\times 3$

$=$ ______

d $22 \times 23 =$ ______ $\times$ ______ $\times 23$

$=$ ______ $\times$ ______

$=$ ______

3 Jake found the product of 15×48 by using factors like this:

$15 \times 48 = 5 \times 3 \times 2 \times 8 \times 3$

$= 10 \times 9 \times 8$

$= 90 \times 8$

$= 720$

Use factors to find these products.

a $35 \times 18 =$ ____________

$=$ ____________

$=$ ______

b $14 \times 25 =$ ____________

$=$ ____________

$=$ ______

c $15 \times 96 =$ ____________

$=$ ____________

$=$ ______

d $45 \times 48 =$ ____________

$=$ ____________

$=$ ______

Using closely related facts

Name ....

Let's practise

1 Complete the multiplications using the numbers on the right. Make each one different.

51 × 17 = ________   △ × □ = ________

△ × □ = ________   △ × □ = ________

△ × □ = ________   △ × □ = ________

△ × □ = ________   △ × □ = ________

Let's solve problems

2 Complete the table.

Item	Cost for 1	Cost for 50	Cost for 49	Cost for 51
Crisps	32p	£16		
Sports drink	56p	£28		
Blank CD	72p			
Magazine	95p			
Tennis ball	99p			

Let's investigate

3 Choose a 2-digit number.
Multiply your number by 39 and 41 and write the answers.

___ × 39 = ________   ___ × 41 = ________

What number is half way between the 2 answers? ________

Multiply your original number by 40 and write the answer. ___ × 40 = ________

Write about what you notice.
Investigate using other 2-digit numbers.

? What if you multiplied by 49 and 51?

Multiplying and dividing mentally

Activity Sheet 32

Name ....

Let's solve problems

1

a $1{\cdot}4 \times 10 =$ _____ b $7{\cdot}51 \times 100 =$ _____ c $2{\cdot}9 \times 100 =$ _____

d $63 \div 10 =$ _____ e $9 \div 100 =$ _____ f $4{\cdot}7 \div 100 =$ _____

2 Complete the patterns.

a $38 \times 2 =$ _____ b $16 \div 2 =$ _____ c $25 \times 0{\cdot}5 =$ _____

$3{\cdot}8 \times 2 =$ _____ $1{\cdot}6 \div 2 =$ _____ $2{\cdot}5 \times 0{\cdot}5 =$ _____

$0{\cdot}38 \times 2 =$ _____ $0{\cdot}16 \div 2 =$ _____ $0{\cdot}25 \times 0{\cdot}5 =$ _____

Let's investigate

3 Lia investigates consecutive numbers using this diagram.

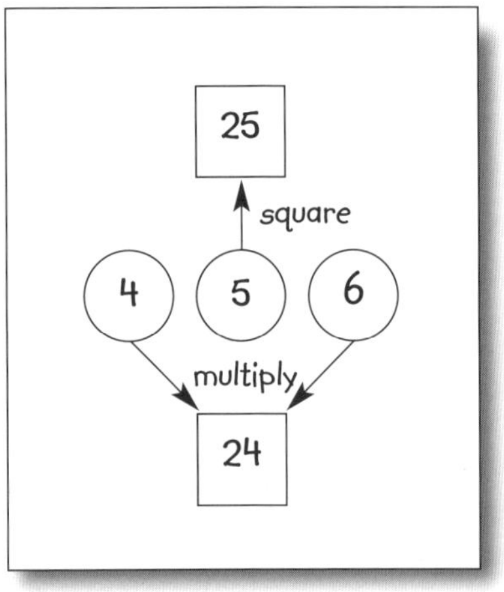

Investigate what Lia says by completing these diagrams.
Choose your own sets of 3 consecutive numbers.

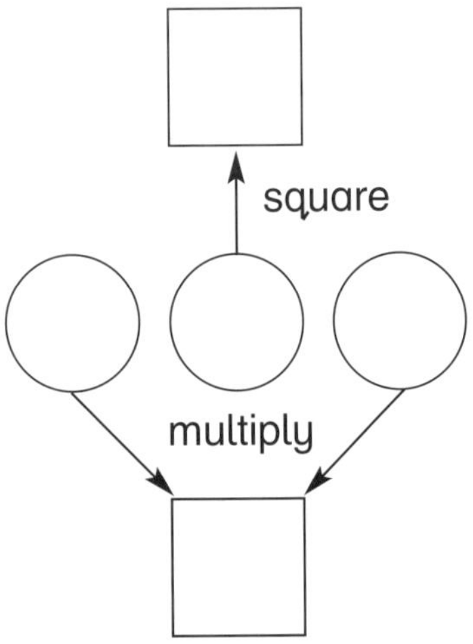

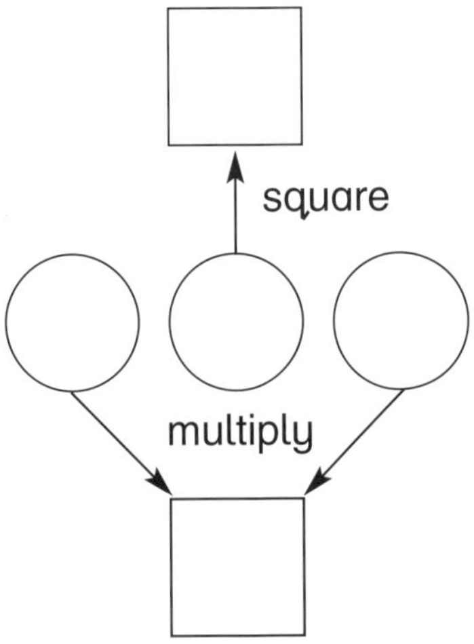

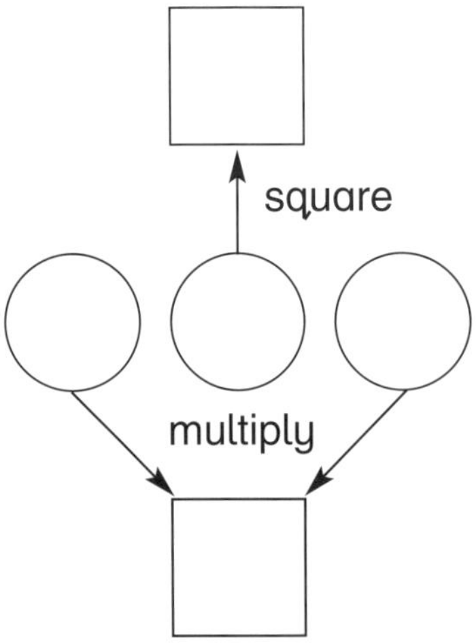

? What if the 3 'consecutive' numbers were 3·9, 4·0 and 4·1?

Multiplying decimals

Activity Sheet 33

Name ....

Let's practise

1 Complete the tables.

Multiplication	Approximate answer	Exact answer
4·2 × 5		
5·3 × 4		
6·6 × 6		
7·8 × 8		

Multiplication	Approximate answer	Exact answer
11·7 × 9		
13·2 × 7		
15·8 × 6		
17·3 × 8		

2 Help Sunil with his homework. Mark each multiplication with a tick or a cross and use the space in the box to correct the wrong answers.

a 3·25 × 4 = 13 ☐
b 5·72 × 6 = 33·42 ☐
c 7·93 × 5 = 40·65 ☐
d 8·06 × 7 = 56·42 ☐
e 9·48 × 8 = 75·84 ☐
f 8·74 × 9 = 78·56 ☐

Let's investigate

3 Use the digits 4 5 6 7 to complete the decimal multiplications.

Investigate making larger and larger answers.

☐·☐☐ × ☐ = ______   ☐·☐☐ × ☐ = ______
☐·☐☐ × ☐ = ______   ☐·☐☐ × ☐ = ______
☐·☐☐ × ☐ = ______   ☐·☐☐ × ☐ = ______
☐·☐☐ × ☐ = ______   ☐·☐☐ × ☐ = ______
☐·☐☐ × ☐ = ______   ☐·☐☐ × ☐ = ______
☐·☐☐ × ☐ = ______   ☐·☐☐ × ☐ = ______

? What if the multiplications were ☐☐·☐ × ☐ using the same 4 digits?

Using long multiplication (2)

Name ....

Let's practise

1

a

	7	3	2
×		2	7

b

	8	3	2
×		3	8

c

	9	3	2
×		4	9

2 Find the missing digit. Use the box to show how you did it.

a 32☐ × 23 = 7498

b 254 × 1☐ = 4826

c 40☐ × 28 = 11 452

d 453 × ☐4 = 15 402

Let's investigate

3 Investigate products of a 3-digit and a 2-digit number that all have the answer 58 212.

_____ × ____ = 58 212 _____ × ____ = 58 212 _____ × ____ = 58 212

_____ × ____ = 58 212 _____ × ____ = 58 212 _____ × ____ = 58 212

? What if the product of a 4-digit number multiplied by a 1-digit number was 58 212?

Using short division (2)

Name ....

You need
coloured pencils

Let's practise

1 Complete the table.

Division	Approximate answer	Exact answer as a mixed number	Multiplication check
188 ÷ 6			
254 ÷ 9			
249 ÷ 6			
342 ÷ 7			
295 ÷ 8			
443 ÷ 7			

2
- Colour a number in the circle.
- Find the number from the square that, when divided into your coloured number, will give the answer closest to 40.
- Continue until all the numbers in the circle are coloured.

256	369
147	310

6	7
8	9

Which of the 16 divisions gives the answer closest to 40? ________

Let's play   A game for 2

You need
a 0–9 dice

- Take turns to roll the dice.
- Write the digit somewhere in your division.
- Repeat until the division is complete.
- Work out the answer.
- The player with the answer nearer to 100 wins.

	Player 1	Player 2
Game 1	☐) ☐ ☐ ☐	☐) ☐ ☐ ☐
Game 2	☐) ☐ ☐ ☐	☐) ☐ ☐ ☐
Game 3	☐) ☐ ☐ ☐	☐) ☐ ☐ ☐

Solving division problems

Activity Sheet **36**

Name ....

Let's solve problems

You need
coloured pencils

1 Colour the answer in the grids below.

a In the spring, during its return to Britain from Africa, a swallow flies 924 miles in 12 days. How far, on average, does it fly each day?

b A bus makes the same trip 26 times in a day. At the end of the day it has travelled 832 miles. What is the length of each trip?

c I think of a number, multiply it by 43 and the answer is 903. What is my number?

d 666 apples are equally divided into 37 crates. How many apples in each crate?

e The area of a rectangular lawn is 754 m^2. One side is 29 m long. How long is one of the shorter sides?

f I drove 976 miles in 16 hours. What was my average speed in miles per hour?

g A secret number is multiplied by 39. The answer is 975. What is the secret number?

h A farmer puts his 782 cows into 23 fields with the same number of cows in each field. How many cows are in each field?

i At the match, 962 people go into the ground through 13 turnstiles. The same number of people go through each turnstile. How many go through each one?

j 17 people shared equally £986 in a lottery win. How much did each receive?

Look at the squares that are not coloured. What 3-letter word can you see?

73	19	30
18	29	74
21	52	32

17	56	41
12	34	37
£42	22	13

37	61	11
26	65	77
25	41	58

Developing calculator skills

Name ....

Let's practise

1 Write the missing digits to complete these calculations.

a 493□82 + 8□009□ = 130□8□0 **b** □51 × 29□ = 193□47

c 1□71□6 – 3049□ = 86□75 **d** 22□466 ÷ □58 = 62□

Let's solve problems

2 **a** In its first 6 days, the number of CDs sold by a shop doubled every day.
Altogether the shop sold 252 CDs.
How many did it sell each day?

Day 1		Day 2		Day 3		Day 4		Day 5		Day 6	
□	+	□	+	□	+	□	+	□	+	□	= 252

b In another shop, the number of CDs sold halved every day.
Altogether the shop sold 504 CDs in 6 days.
How many did it sell each day?

Day 1		Day 2		Day 3		Day 4		Day 5		Day 6	
□	+	□	+	□	+	□	+	□	+	□	= 504

3 **a** Arrange these numbers into 3 sets of 3 so that the total of each set is 650.

332	204	312
101	83	162
255	217	284

b Make up a puzzle like this one for a friend to solve.

Miles and kilometres

Activity Sheet 38

Name ....

Let's practise

5 miles ≈ 8 km

1 Complete the table.

Miles	Kilometres
0	
5	8
10	
15	24
20	
25	
30	

A miles/kilometres conversion graph

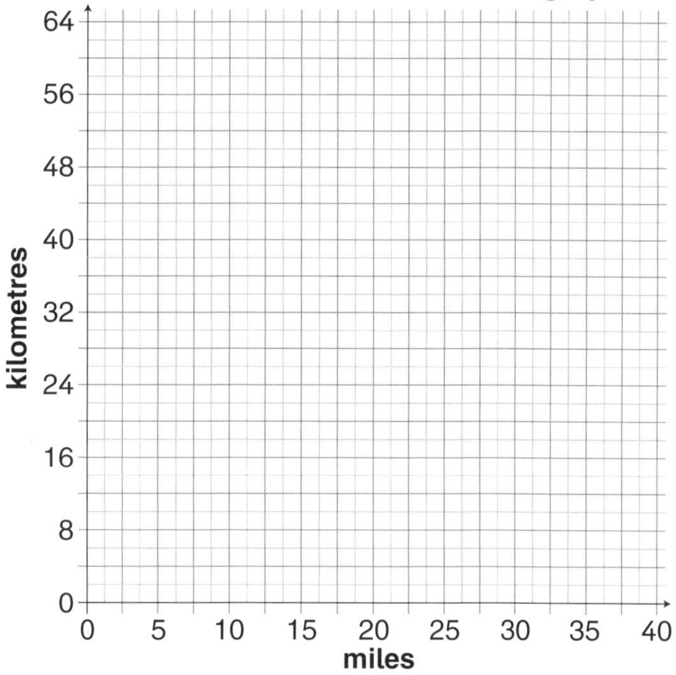

2 Use your table from question 1.
Plot the points on the graph.
Join them in a straight line.
Continue it as far as you can.

3 Use your graph to convert these distances.

a 40 km ≈ _____ miles **b** 40 miles ≈ _____ km **c** 64 km ≈ _____ miles

d 12 km ≈ _____ miles **e** 17·5 miles ≈ _____ km **f** 22·5 miles ≈ _____ km

4 Write each distance in kilometres, to the nearest km, then in miles.

7940 m = 7·94 km
≈ 8 km
≈ 5 miles

a 3890 m = _____ km
≈ _____ km
≈ _____ miles

b 11 700 m = _____ km
≈ _____ km
≈ _____ miles

Let's solve problems

5 **a** The signpost shows distances in miles. How far is it in kilometres from

- Scotch Corner to Penrith _____ km
- Bowes to Appleby? _____ km

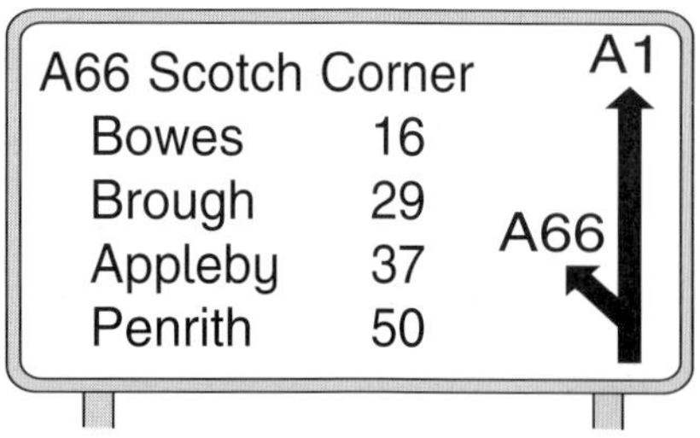

b You are on the A66, 44 km past Scotch Corner.
What is your nearest town? ______________

Grams and ounces

Activity Sheet **39**

Name ....

Let's practise

1 Use the graph to convert these masses.
Round your answers to the nearest ounce or 25 g.

a 2 oz ≈ ______ g **b** 60 g ≈ ______ oz

c 7 oz ≈ ______ g **d** 375 g ≈ ______ oz

e 9 oz ≈ ______ g **f** 225 g ≈ ______ oz

g 16 oz ≈ ______ g **h** 425 g ≈ ______ oz

An ounces/grams conversion graph

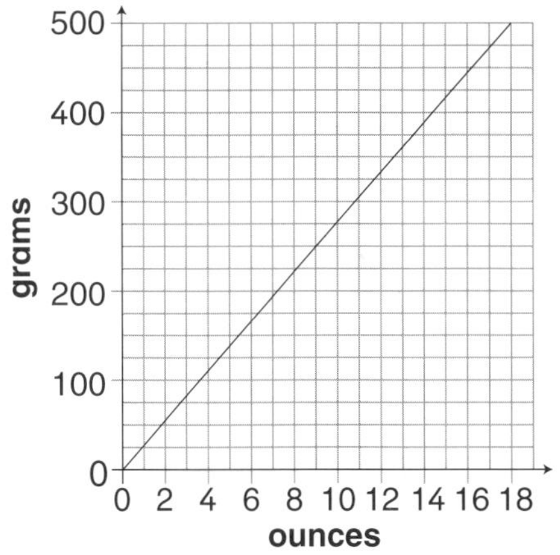

2 Write > or < to make each statement true.

a 4 oz ☐ 100 g **b** 13 oz ☐ 350 g

c 6 oz ☐ 175 g **d** 14 oz ☐ 400 g

Let's solve problems

3 The imperial system uses these standard masses:
1 oz, 2 oz, 4 oz, 8 oz, 16 oz, 32 oz, 64 oz, ….

Find the smallest number of masses you need to balance these amounts.

	1 oz	2 oz	4 oz	8 oz	16 oz	32 oz	64 oz	Check
28 oz			✓	✓	✓			4 + 8 + 16 = 28
19 oz								
41 oz								
53 oz								
4 lb								

4 The referee suspects that one of these 16 snooker balls is lighter than the others. He uses a pan balance to compare them. What is the least number of times he must balance the balls to find the odd one out?
Show how you solved the problem.

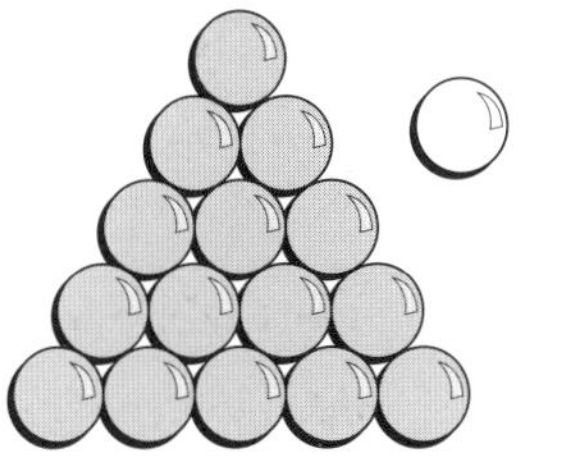

Litres, pints and gallons (2)

Activity Sheet 40

Name ....

Let's solve problems

You need
coloured pencils

Find how much fuel the winning car used by following these steps. Colour squares as you eliminate them.

Step 1 Eliminate all litres approximately equal to 1, 2, 3, 4, 5 or 6 gallons.
Step 2 Eliminate all gallons less than 45 litres.
Step 3 Eliminate all pints less than 5 gallons.
Step 4 Eliminate all amounts that are square numbers.
Step 5 Eliminate all litres with the last 2 digits divisible by 4.

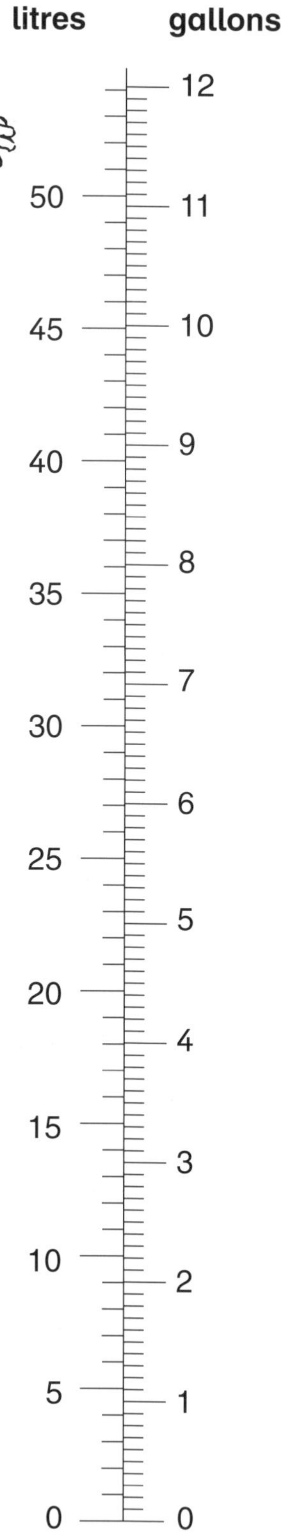

4·5 l	49 l	22·5 l	5 gallons	12·64 l	13 pints
6 gallons	3·48 l	25 pints	13·5 l	37 pints	16 gallons
36 gallons	9 l	3 gallons	43·6 l	50 l	0·96 l
1·24 l	30 pints	81 l	4 pints	18 l	27 pints
23 pints	7 gallons	27·2 l	10 pints	2 gallons	27 l
8 gallons	37·6 l	64 l	9 gallons	32 pints	100 pints

The amount you have not eliminated is the answer.

Write it here. ______________

Perimeter puzzles

Activity Sheet 41

Name ....

Let's solve problems

1
- Cut out the 4 L-shapes below.
- Arrange the L-shapes to make each polygon in turn. Show their outlines on each diagram.
- Find the perimeter of each polygon.

You need

1 cm square dotty paper, scissors, a ruler

a
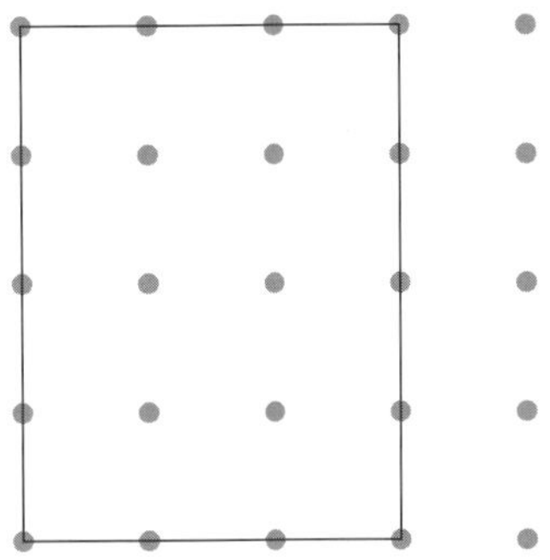
P = _______ cm

b
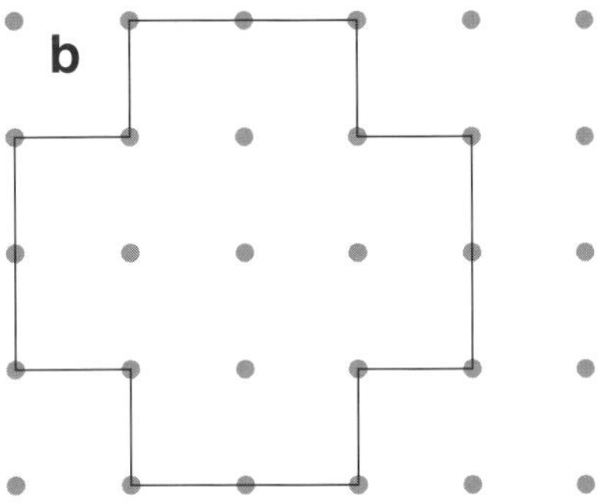
P = _______ cm

c
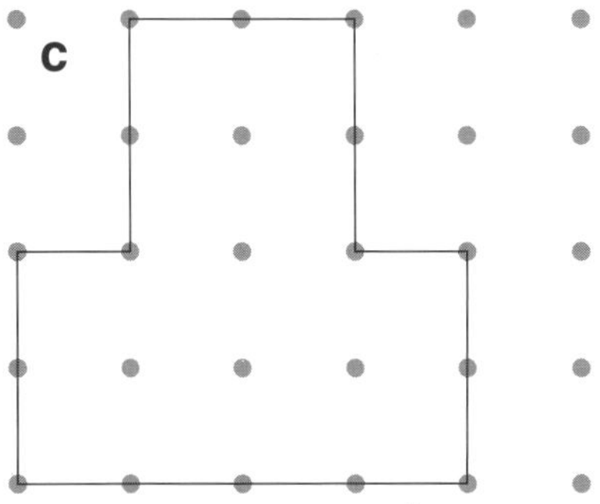
P = _______ cm

d
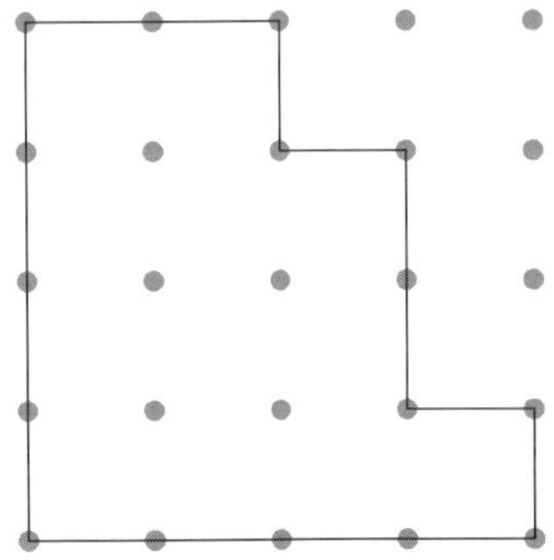
P = _______ cm

e
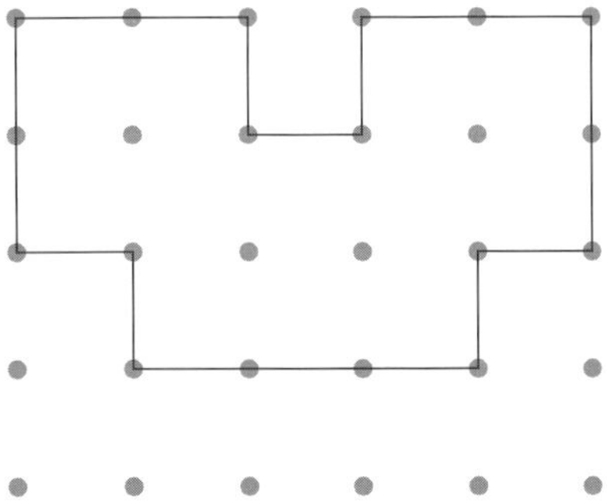
P = _______ cm

f
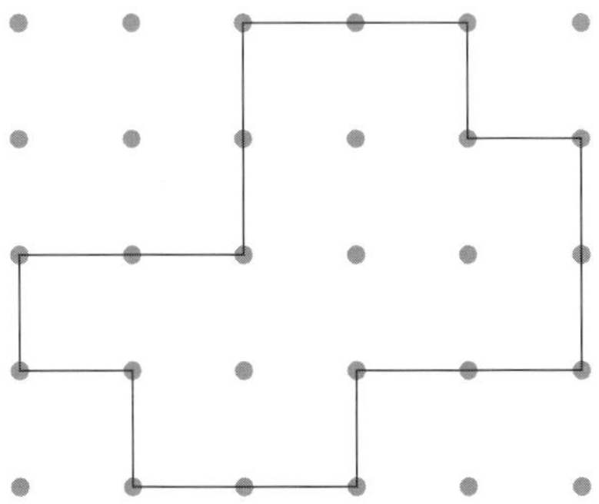
P = _______ cm

Let's investigate

2 Fit the L-shapes together to make different polygons. Draw each polygon you make on 1 cm square dotty paper and record its perimeter. Find the polygons with the longest and shortest perimeters.

? What if you had 5 L-shapes?

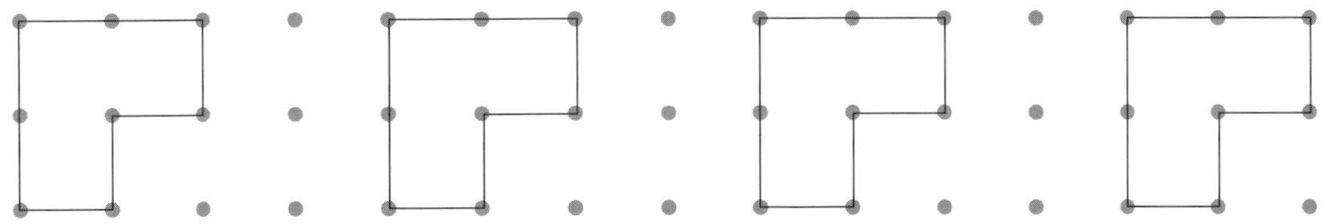

Times around the world (1)

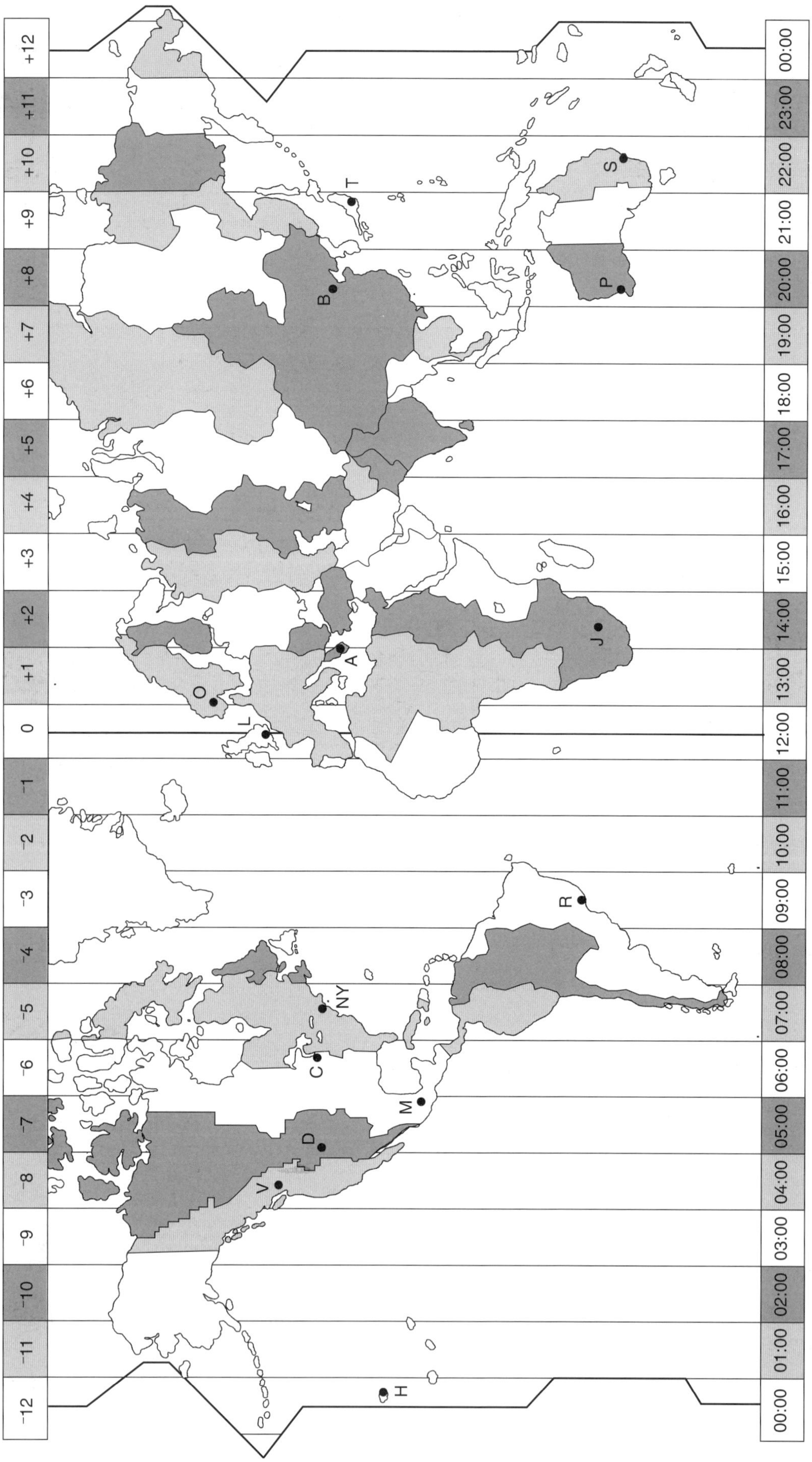

Key

A Athens
B Beijing
C Chicago
D Denver
H Hawaii
J Johannesburg
L London
M Mexico City
NY New York
O Oslo
P Perth
R Rio de Janeiro
S Sydney
T Tokyo
V Vancouver

Kite and trapezium

Activity Sheet **43**

Name ....

Let's investigate

1 A trapezium has 1 pair of opposite sides parallel.
Draw a different trapezium in each grid.
Mark the parallel sides.

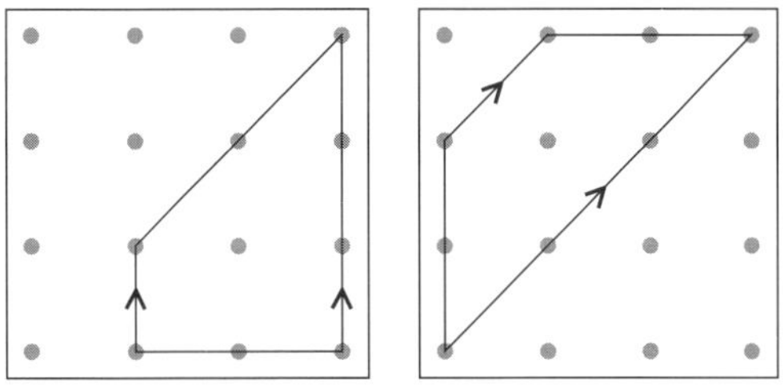

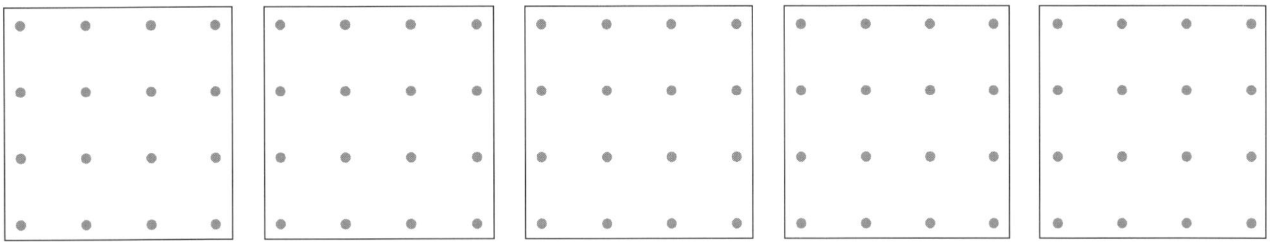

2 Arrowheads and kites have 2 pairs of adjacent sides equal.
Draw a different arrowhead or kite in each grid.
Mark the equal sides.

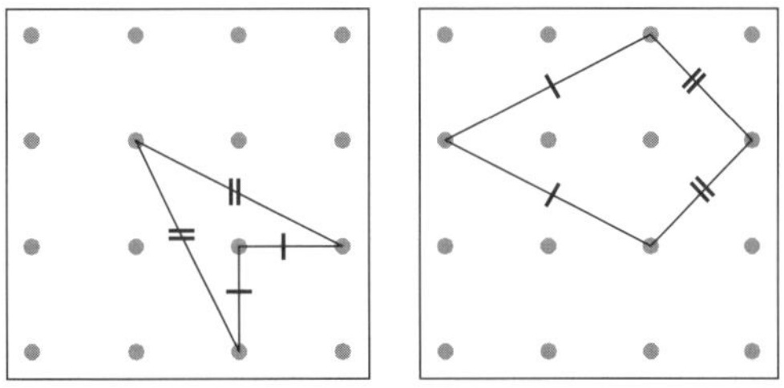

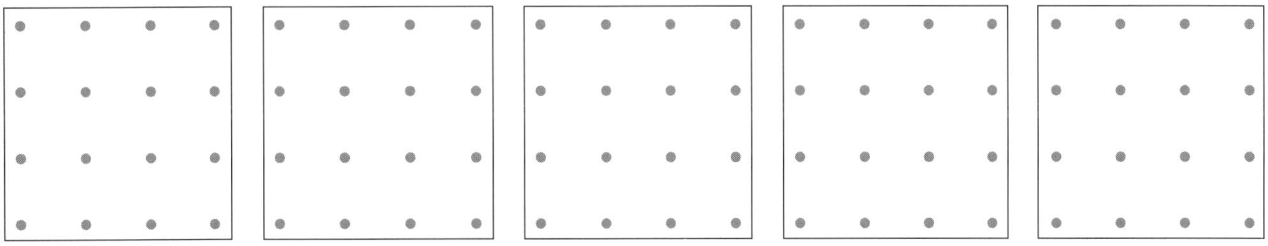

3 Work with a partner.
Follow these steps and make 4 kites each.
Investigate patterns you can make using all 8 kites each time.

You each need
4 sheets of A4 paper
(2 white and 2 coloured)

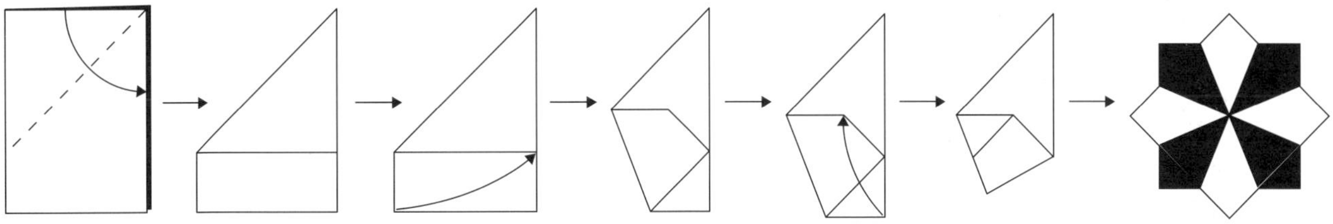

1 kite **8 kites**

Circle patterns

Name ....

Let's investigate

1 The letter *n* represents any numbered point around the circle.

You need 
a ruler

You want to join n to n + 2.
If n = 1, you join 1 to 3.
If n = 6, you join 6 to 8.

a Complete the table for $n \rightarrow n + 2$.

n	1	2	3	4	5	6	7	8
$n + 2$	3					8		

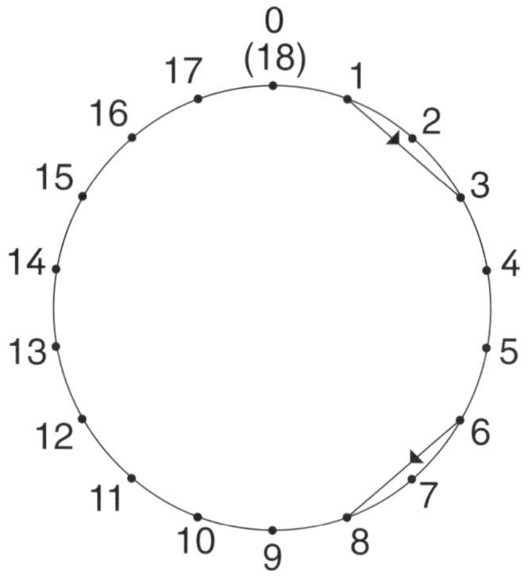

b Complete the line pattern for $n \rightarrow n + 2$.

c Write about what you notice.

____

____

2 Complete the tables and create the line patterns for:

a $n \rightarrow n + 5$

n	1	2	3	4	5	6	7	8
$n + 5$	6							

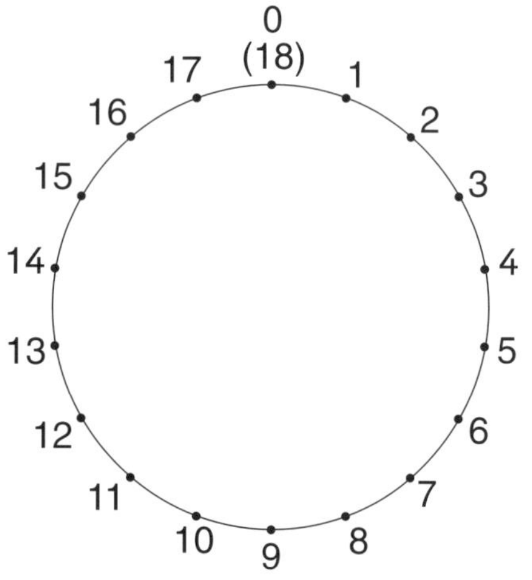

Write about what you notice.

____

____

b $n \rightarrow n + 8$

n	1	2	3	4	5	6	7	8
$n + 8$								

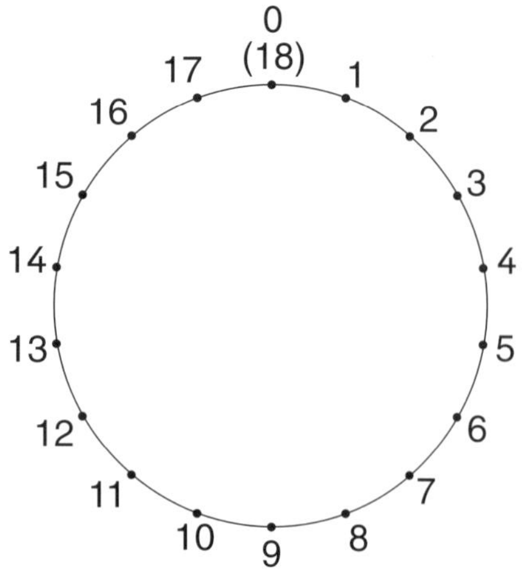

Write about what you notice.

____

____

Diagonals in quadrilaterals

Activity Sheet **45**

Name ....

Let's investigate

You need
a ruler, a pencil,
a red pencil

1

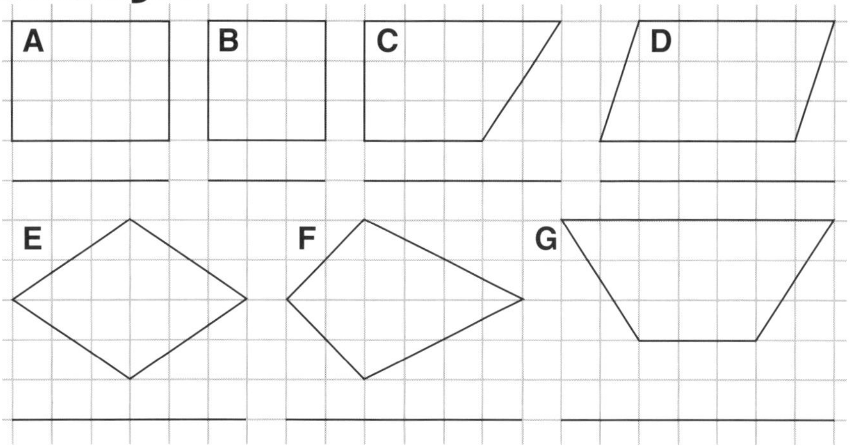

a Write the name of each quadrilateral.

b Carefully rule, in pencil, both diagonals in each quadrilateral.

c Complete the table. Mark ✓ for true and ✗ for false.

Property of diagonals	**Quadrilateral**						
	A	**B**	**C**	**D**	**E**	**F**	**G**
are the same length							
bisect each other							
intersect at right angles							

d Complete this statement about the quadrilaterals:

The diagonals of the ________________, ____________________ and

________________ intersect at right angles.

e Colour red any diagonal that is a line of symmetry.

f Name the shapes with red diagonals. ________________________________

2 Make a general statement about quadrilaterals that have diagonals that bisect each other.

____

____

Finding and using patterns

Name ....

Let's investigate

You need
coloured pencils

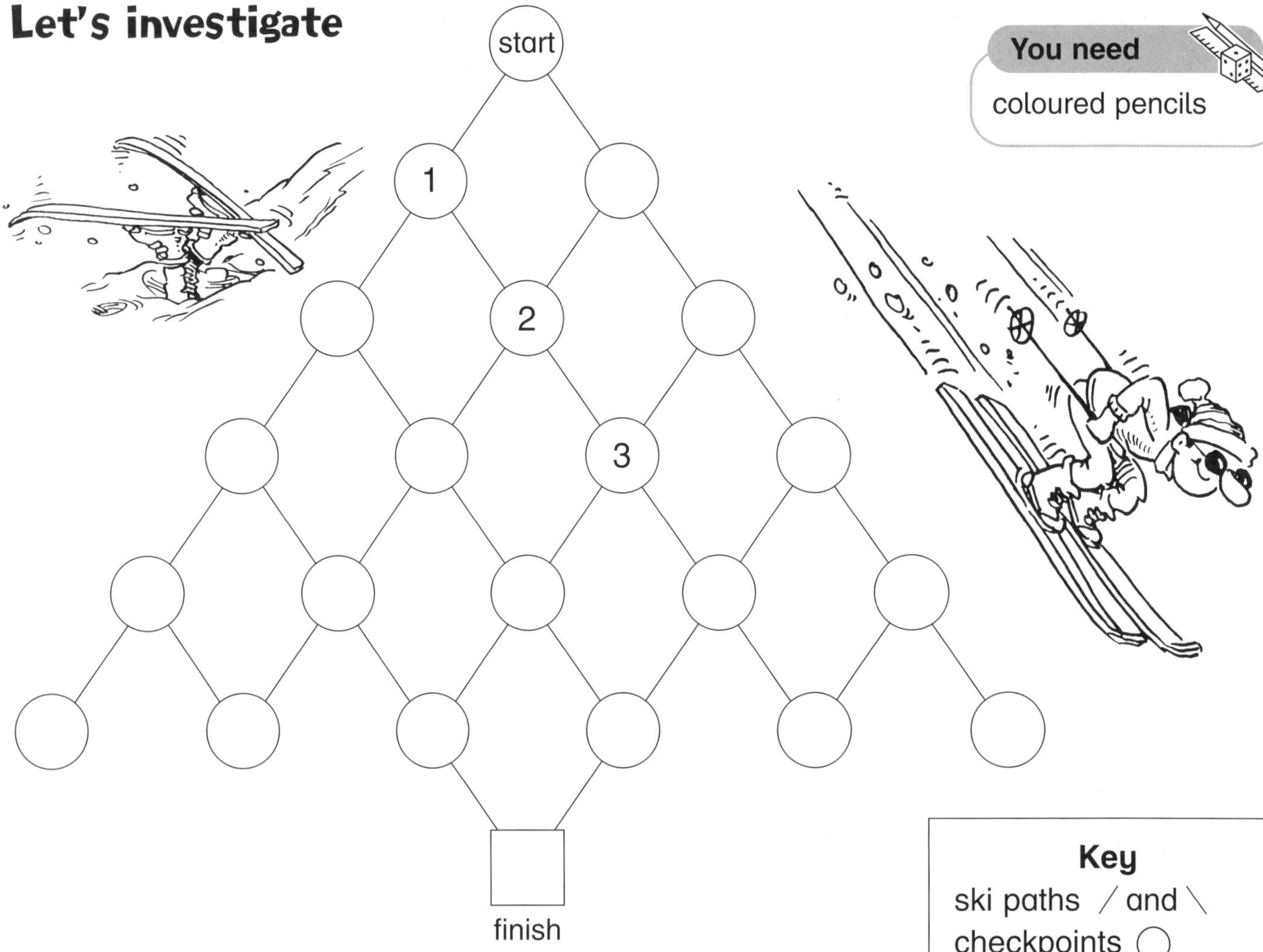

Key
ski paths / and \
checkpoints ◯

There are 2 different paths to the checkpoint with 2 in it.
There are 3 ways to ski to the checkpoint with 3 in it.

1 Start at the top of the mountain.
Draw the 3 ways to ski to checkpoint 3.
Use a different colour for each path.

2 How many different ways are there to ski to each checkpoint?
Write the answer in each circle.

3 Use the pattern to work out how many different ski paths you can take from 'start' to 'finish'.
Write the answer in the 'finish' box.

Symmetry in designs

Name ....

Let's investigate

You need
a ruler, coloured pencils

1 Reflect the Roman mosaic design in both mirror lines.
Use colour to show the reflective symmetry.

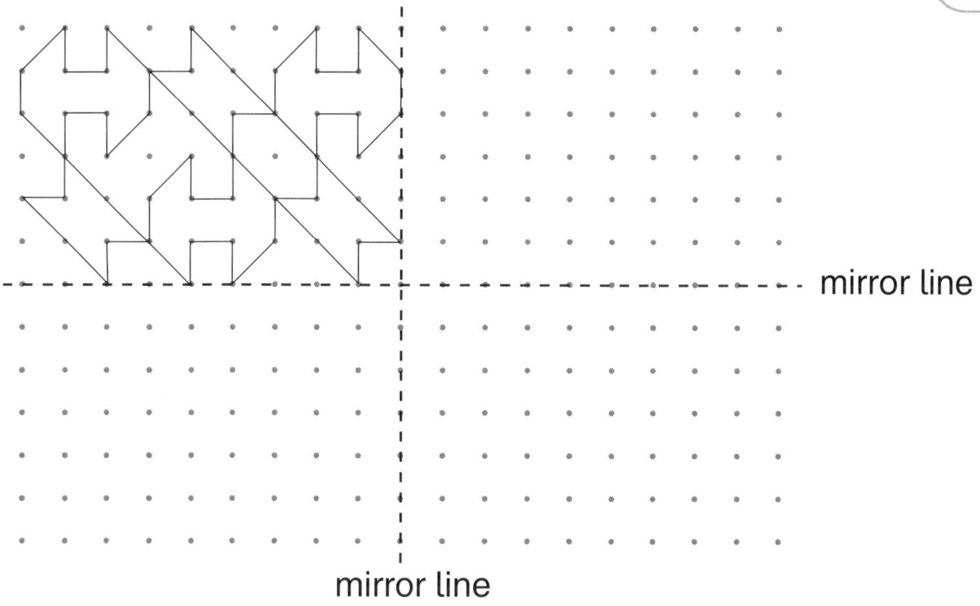

2 Reflect the North American Indian design in both mirror lines.
The design is known as the Navajo Eye Dazzler.
Use colour to show the reflective symmetry.

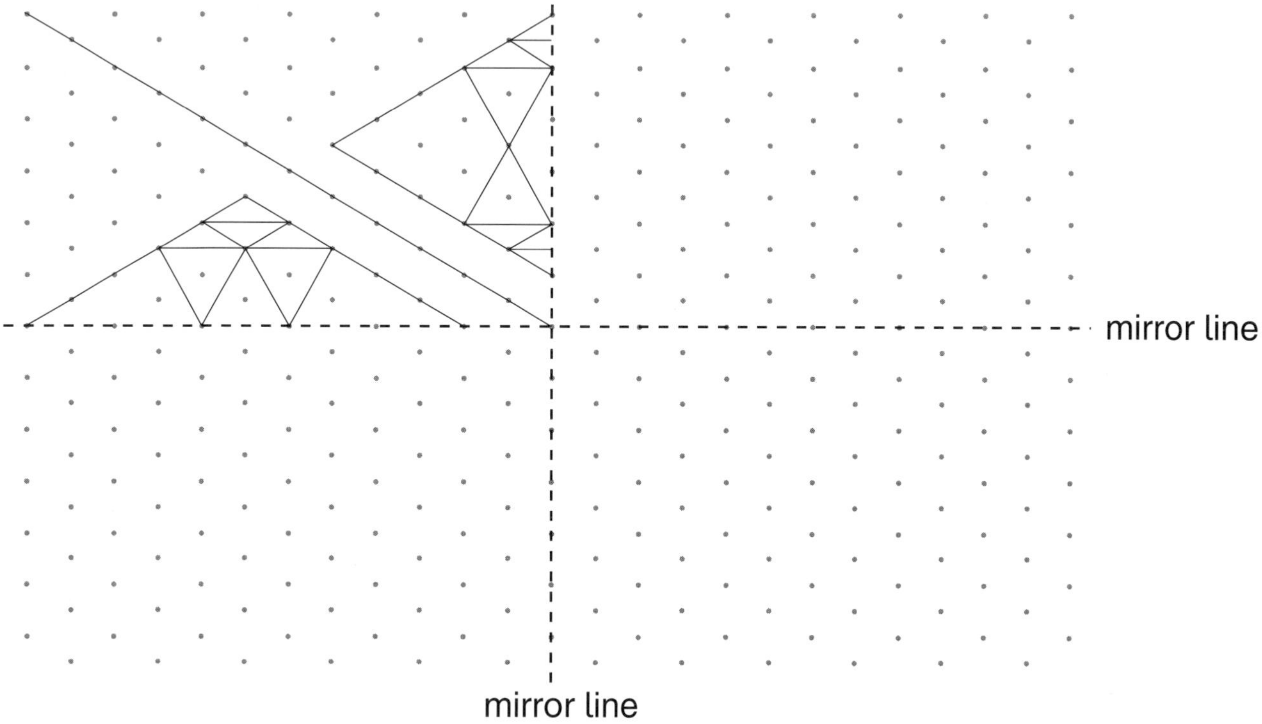

Translating a shape

Activity Sheet 48

Name ....

Let's solve problems

You need
a ruler,
coloured pencils

1 **a** On the same diagram make two translations of each shape:
- 1 unit right, 1 unit down
- 1 unit left, 1 unit up.

b Colour the shape in the overlap. Name the shape.

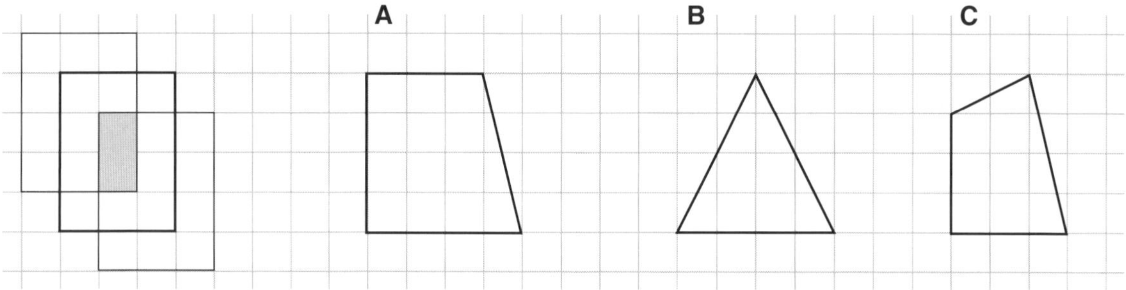

rectangle ____________ ____________ ____________

2 **a** Use diagram 1 below.
- Translate shape **A** 4 units right and 2 units up to make shape **B**.
- The coordinates of the vertices of **B** are (__, __), (__, __), (__, __).

b Use diagram 2 below.
- Plot these points for shape **D**: (4, 4), (5, 3), (5, 1), (2, 1), (2, 3).
- Complete this statement:

Shape **C** has been translated ___ units to the _______ and ___ units _______ to make shape **D**.

Diagram 1

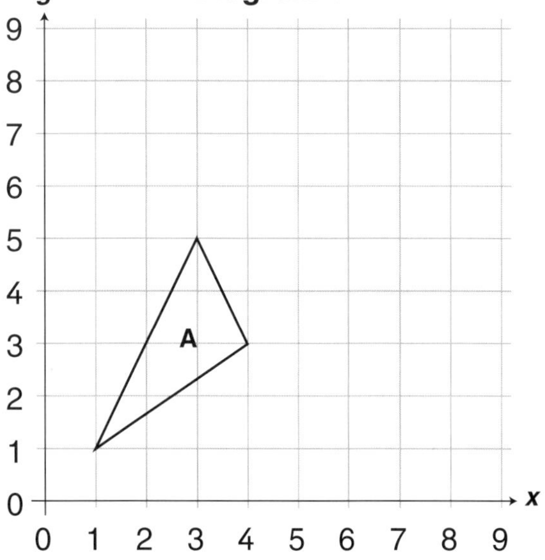

Diagram 2

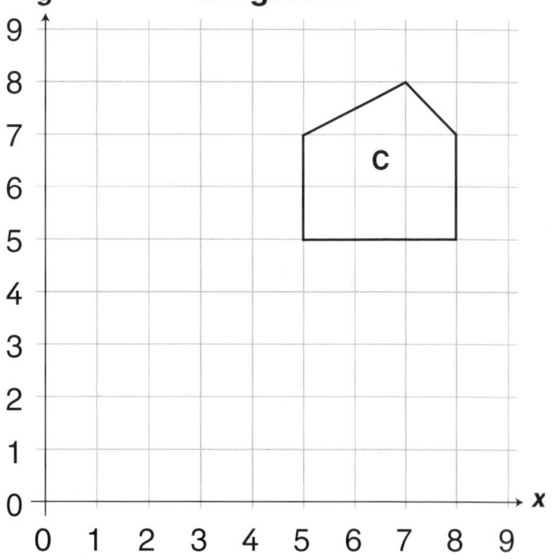

Coordinates of shapes

Name ....

You need
Activity Sheet 50, a ruler

Let's practice

1 Write the coordinates of the vertices of each shape.

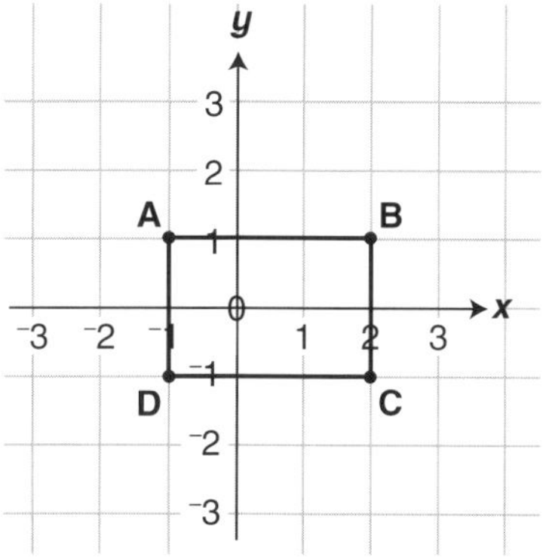

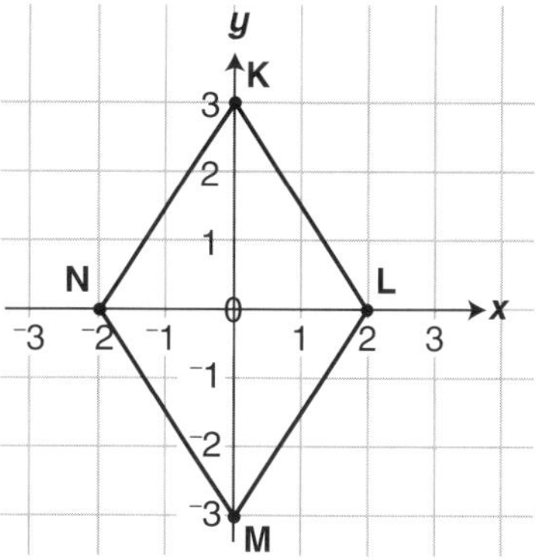

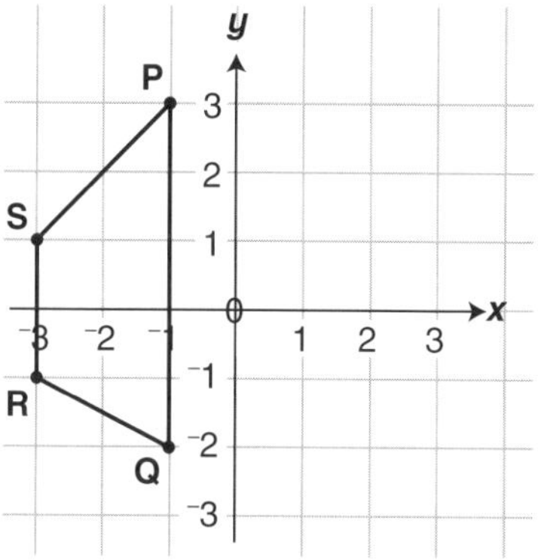

a rectangle ABCD

(__, __), (__, __),

(__, __), (__, __)

b rhombus KLMN

(__, __), (__, __),

(__, __), (__, __)

c trapezium PQRS

(__, __), (__, __),

(__, __), (__, __)

2 **a** Plot these points on Activity Sheet 50:
E (−3, 1), F (5, 5), G (1, −3), and H (−3, −3).
b Join the points in order and name the shape EFGH. ____________________
c Draw the diagonals. Mark the point of intersection J and write its coordinates.
(__, __)

3 **a** Now plot these points:
T (2, 3), U (4, 5), V (4, −3) and W (2, −1).
Join them up in order.
b Reflect the shape TUVW in the *y*-axis.
Name the reflected shape and list its coordinates.

name ____________ coordinates (__, __), (__, __), (__, __), (__, __)

Let's solve problems

4 The points P (−1, 3) and Q (−1, −1) form one side of a square PQRS.
a Plot the points P and Q on Activity Sheet 50.
Find the vertices R and S and write their coordinates. R(__, __), S(__, __)
Join the points in order to make a square.
b Find a different set of vertices for R and S.

Write their coordinates. R(__, __), S(__, __)

4-quadrant grids

Activity Sheet **50**

Name ....

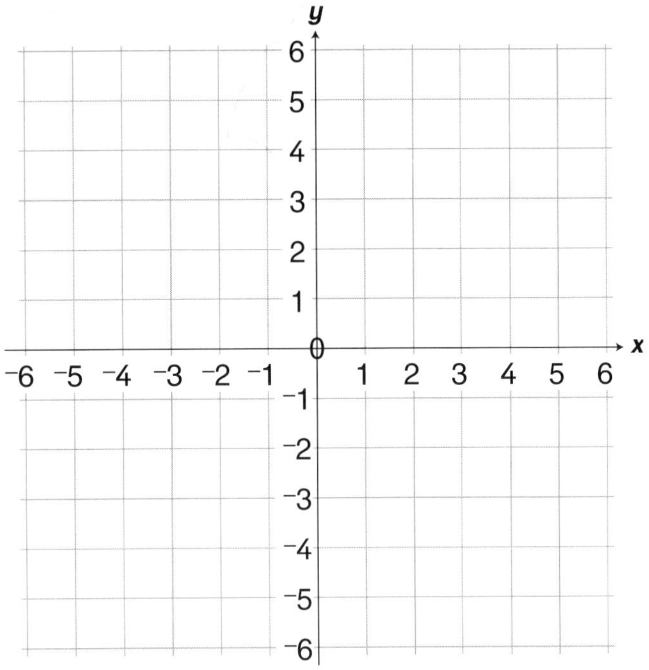

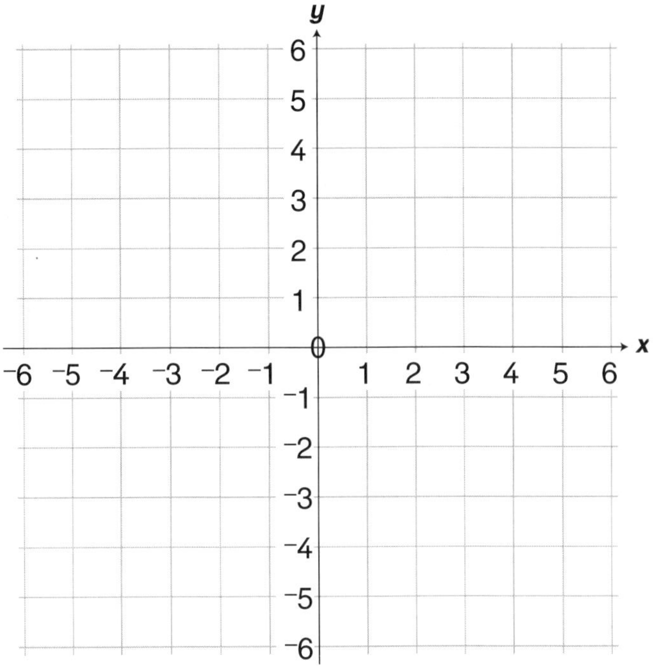

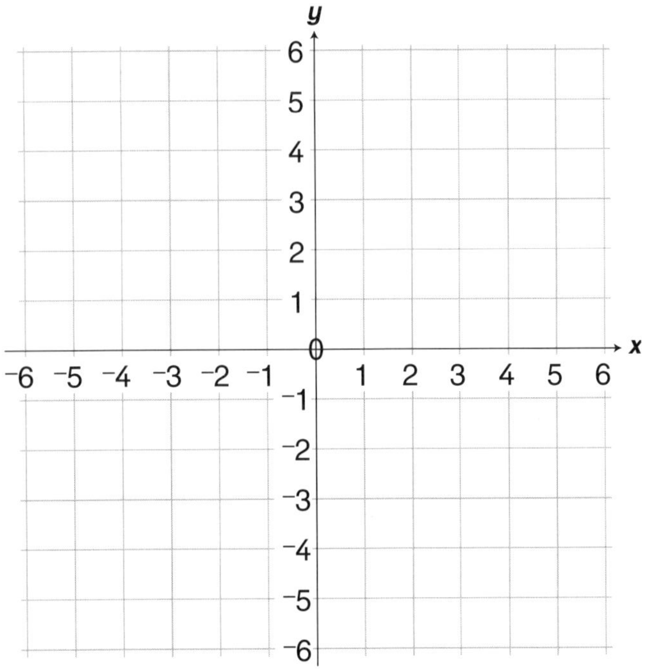

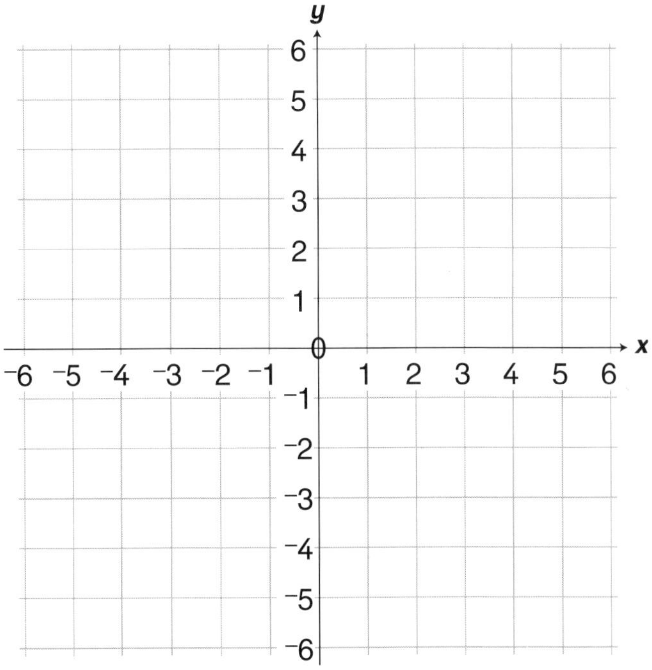

Angles in regular polygons

Name ....

You need

a protractor

Let's investigate

Measure the marked angles to the nearest degree, complete each table and answer the questions.

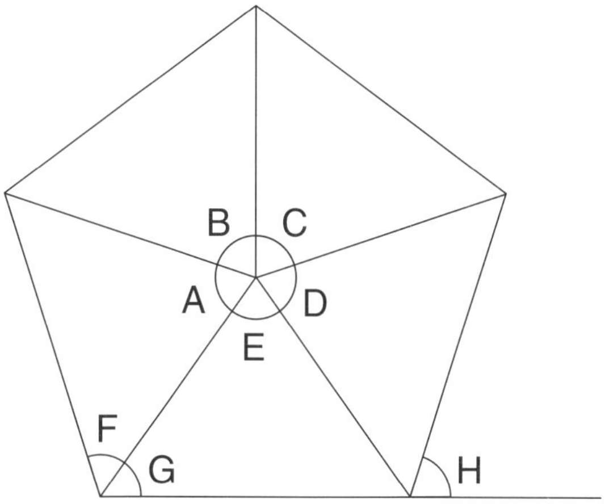

1 a

Angle	A	B	C	D	E	F	G	H
Degrees								

b Find the total of these angles in degrees:

A + B + C + D + E = _____ °

F + G + H = _____ °

2

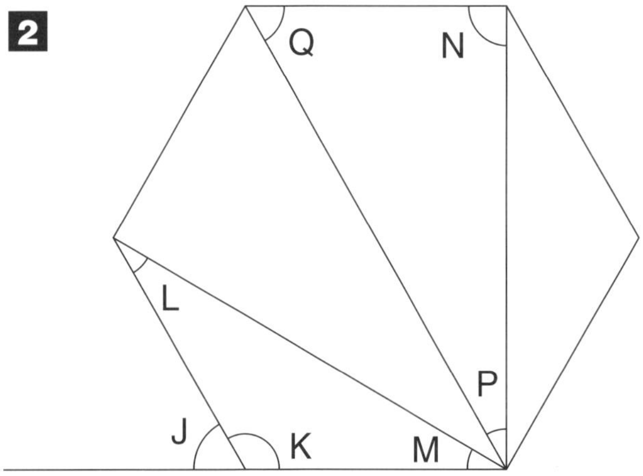

a

Angle	J	K	L	M	N	P	Q
Degrees							

b Find the total of these angles in degrees:

P + Q = _____ °   J + K = _____ °

3 a

Angle	R	S	T	U	V	W	X
Degrees							

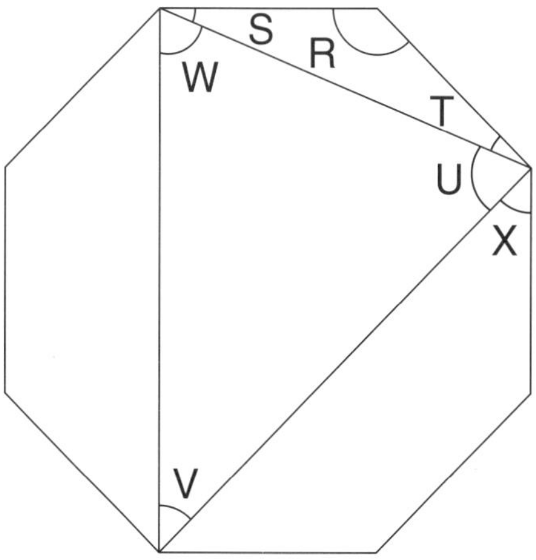

b Find the total of these angles in degrees:

R + S + T = _____ °

U + V + W = _____ °

c Mark in the octagon all the angles that are the same size as angle V.

4 Write about what you have discovered in questions 1 to 3.

Rotating shapes

Name ....

Let's solve problems

1 Rotate each shape through 90° about vertex A.
Repeat the rotation 2 more times.
Write the coordinates of the images of vertex C in each quadrant.

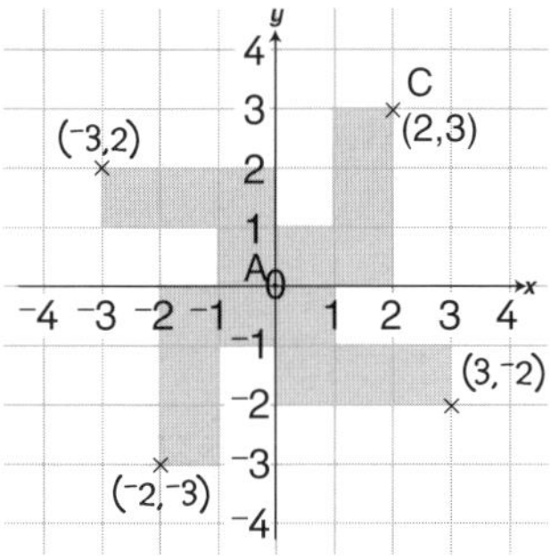

You need
a ruler,
coloured pencils

a

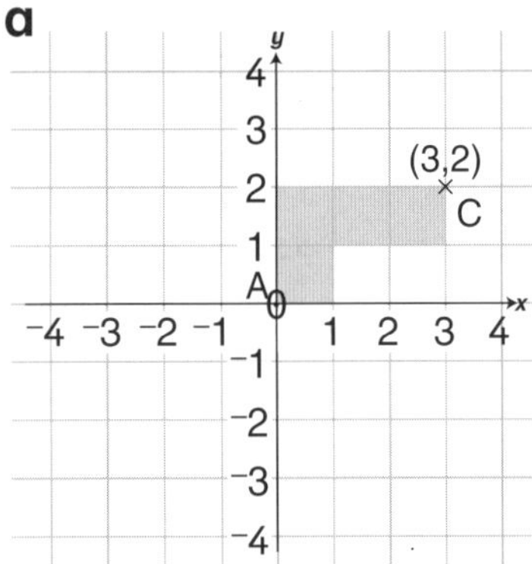

b

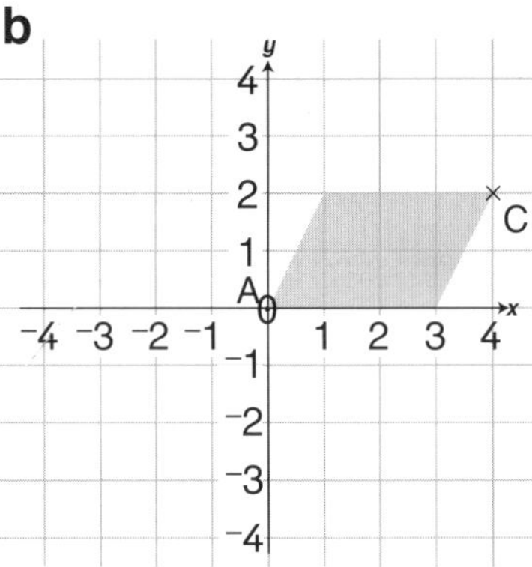

c

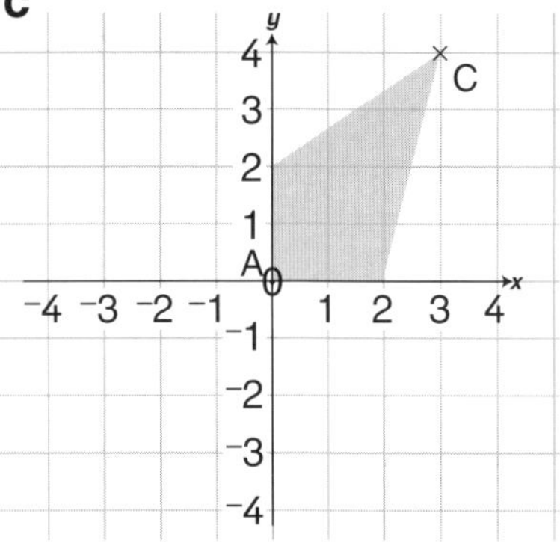

2 Rotate each shape through 90° about the point O. Repeat the rotation 2 more times.
Colour the shapes so each design has rotational symmetry.

a

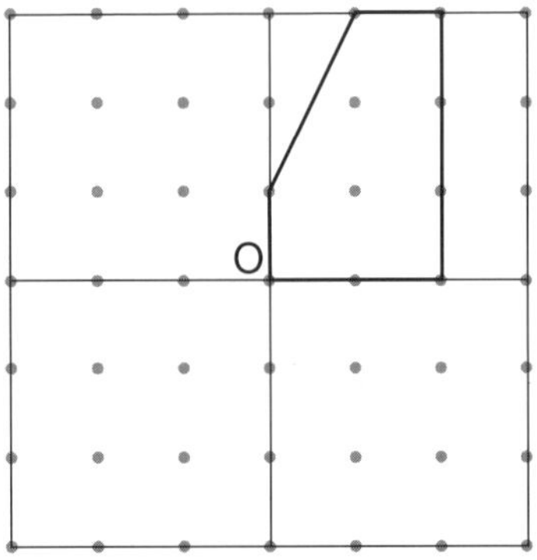

b

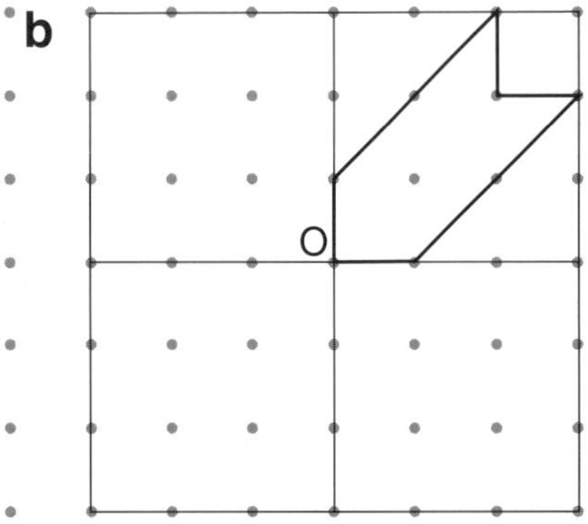

c

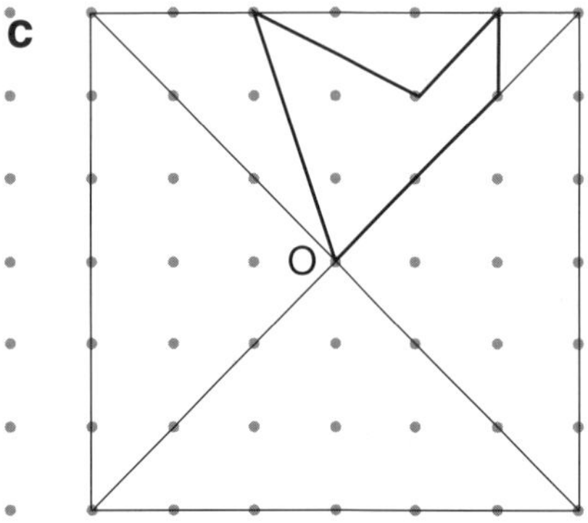

3 Rotate each shape through 60° about the point O. Repeat the rotation 4 more times.
Colour the shapes so each design has rotational symmetry.

a

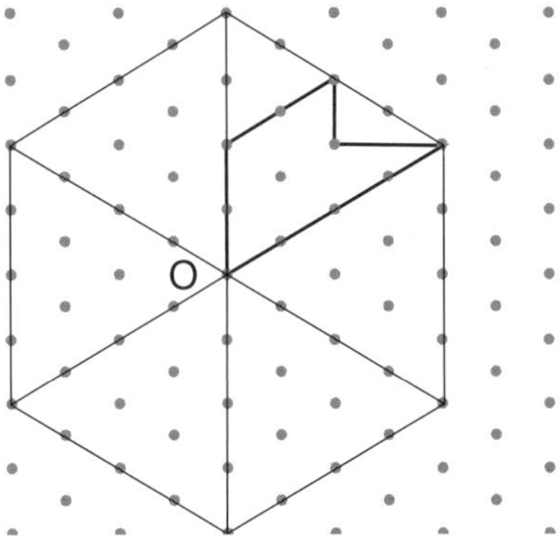

b

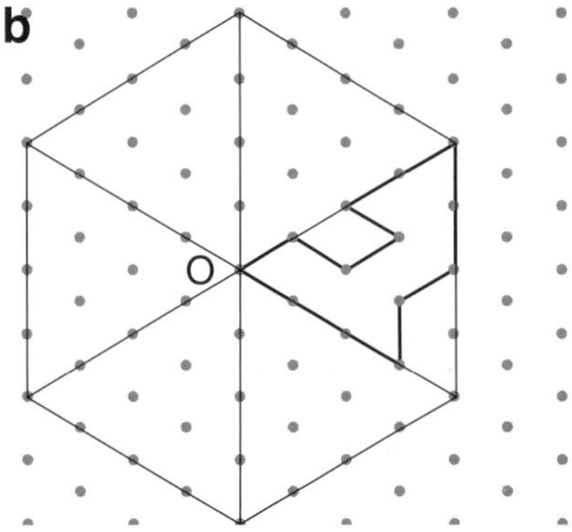

c

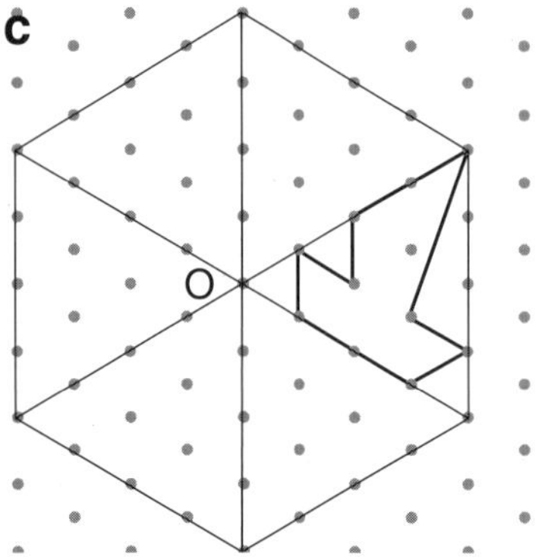

Considering likelihood

Name ....

Let's solve problems

1 Tick the statement that is more likely in each pair.

On a 1–6 dice you will roll a number less than 5.	OR	On a 1–6 dice you will roll a number more than 5.
You will go to the Moon one day.	OR	You will go to the shop this week.
It will snow next winter.	OR	It will snow next week.

2 Write three pairs of statements where one is more likely than the other.

About you		OR	
About your class		OR	
About your school		OR	

Let's play A game for 2

You need

a dice, a small counter each

- Decide who is 'odd' and who is 'even'.
- Take turns to roll the dice.
- If the number is odd, then 'odd' moves their counter one space along the 'odd' line.
- If the number is even, then 'even' moves their counter one space along the 'even' line.
- The first to the other end is the winner.

Odd										

Even										

? What if a coin is tossed and one player is 'heads' and the other is 'tails'?

Expected and experimental probability (coins)

Activity Sheet 54

Name ....

Let's investigate
Work with a partner.

You need
20 counters, a coin

1 Take turns to:

- Put a counter in the labelled start box.
- Before you toss the coin, predict the outcome.
- Toss the coin and move your counter downwards, following the correct arrow.
- Your partner records your prediction (P) and the outcome (O) in the table.
- Predict, toss and record again. Move your counter once more and leave it in the rectangle, the circle or the triangle.

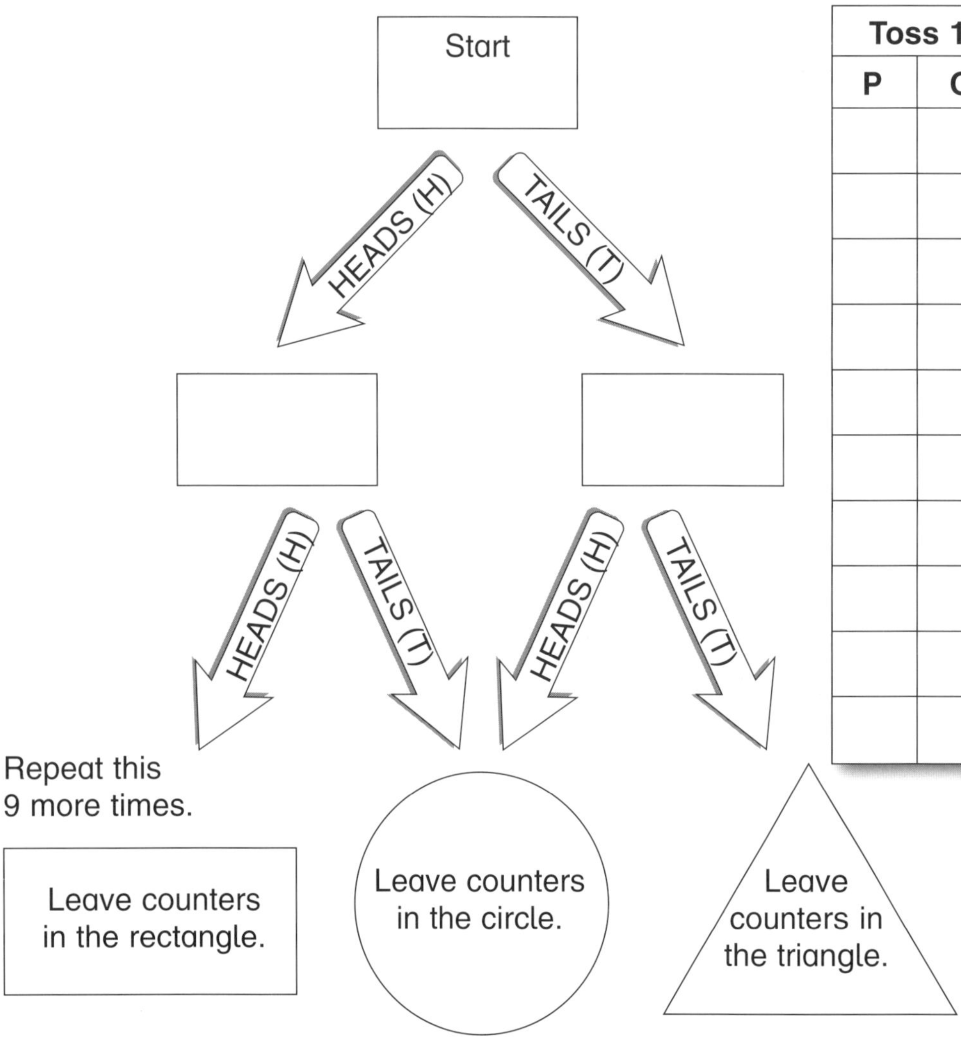

Toss 1		Toss 2		Box
P	**O**	**P**	**O**	

2 Draw an arrow on the probability scale to show the probability of a counter ending up in the rectangle box in question 1. Do the same for the circle and triangle boxes.

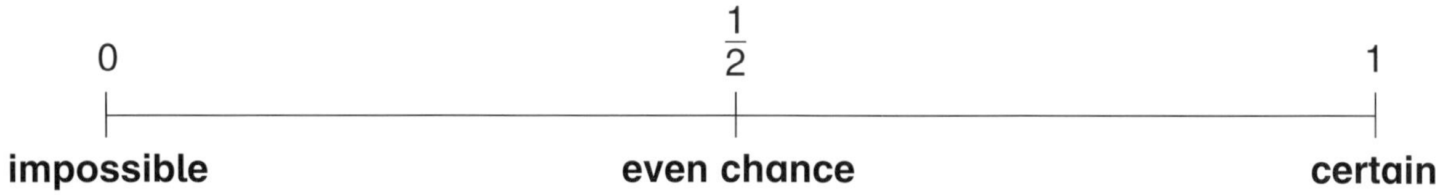

Expected and experimental probability (spinners)

Activity Sheet **55**

Name ....

Let's investigate

You need

a paper clip

Work with a partner.

1 To use the spinner:

- Place the clip in the middle of the spinner.
- Put the point of a pencil inside the clip and touching the middle of spinner.
- Flick the clip around the pencil.

- Take turns to flick the clip around the spinner.
- Put a tally mark by the number that the clip stops spinning at.
- Do 30 flicks each.

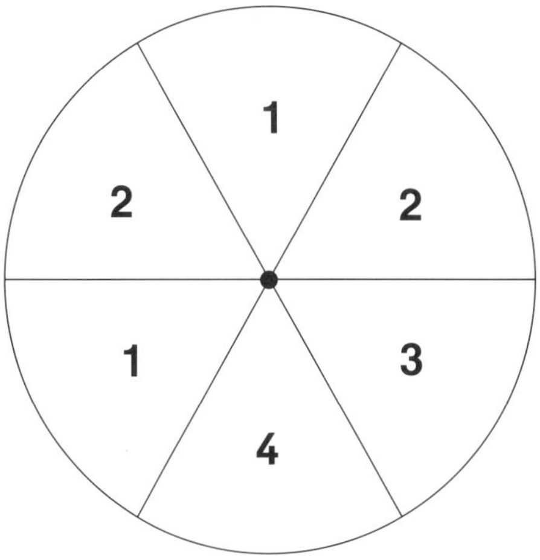

Number	Frequency	Total
1		
2		
3		
4		

2 Write each number 1 to 4 on the probability scale to show the experimental probability of scoring each number.

0 ———————— $\frac{1}{2}$ ———————— **1**

impossible — **even chance** — **certain**

3 Record the expected probability for each number as a fraction.

Probability of 1 is ______ Probability of 2 is ______

Probability of 3 is ______ Probability of 4 is ______

Using straight line graphs (1)

Activity Sheet 56

Name ....

Let's solve problems

You need
a ruler, a sharp pencil

1 On the same grid draw the graphs of the 3×, 4×, 6×, 7×, 8× and 9× tables by plotting the points you already know, then joining them and extending the line as far as you can.

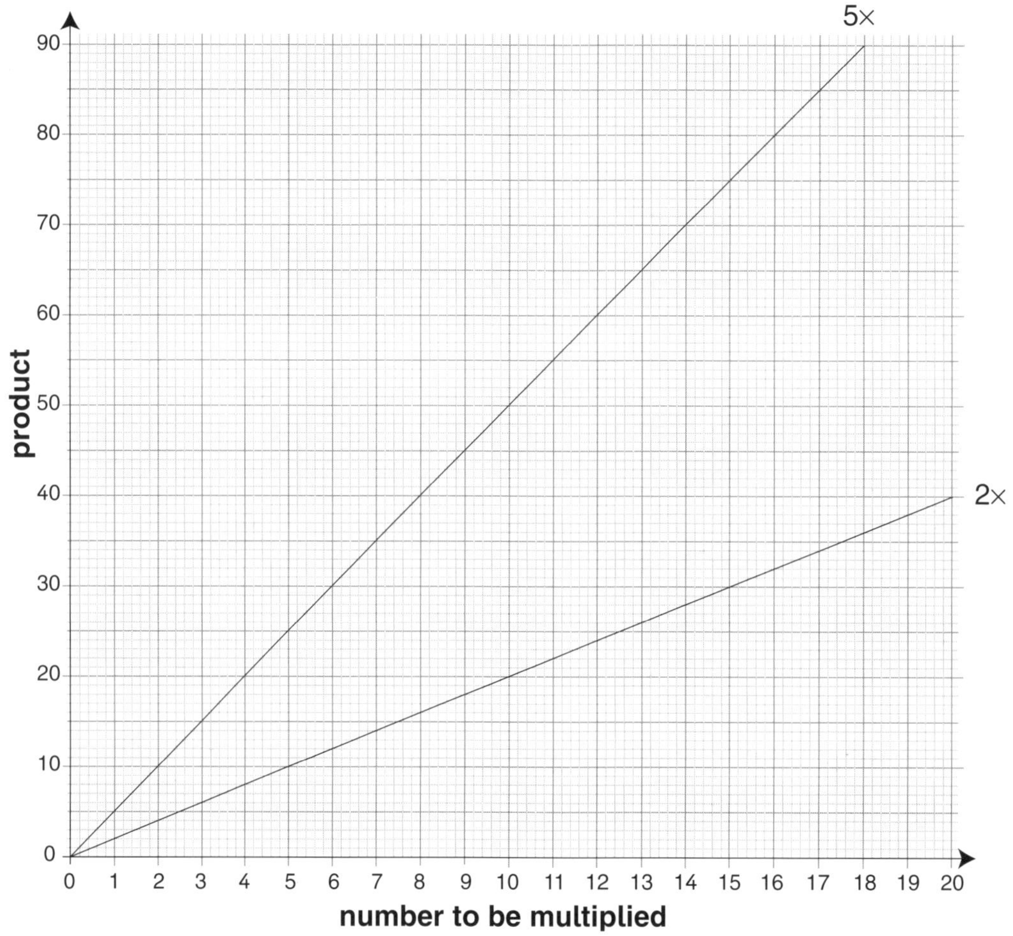

2 Use the graphs to find

a $13 \times 6 =$ _____ **b** $18 \times 4 =$ _____ **c** $3 \times 19 =$ _____ **d** $5 \times 17 =$ _____

3 Plot the products of $2\frac{1}{2} \times 4$, $2\frac{1}{2} \times 8$ and $2\frac{1}{2} \times 10$.

Join the points to make the graph of the '$2\frac{1}{2} \times$ table'.

Use the graph to complete **a** $2\frac{1}{2} \times 6 =$ _____ **b** $2\frac{1}{2} \times 9 =$ _____ **c** $16 \times 2\frac{1}{2} =$ _____

Let's investigate

4 Investigate how you might use the graph to complete

a $7 \times 3\frac{1}{2} =$ _____ **b** $4 \times 8\frac{3}{4} =$ _____ **c** $9 \times 6{\cdot}2 =$ _____

Using a frequency table

Activity Sheet **57**

Name ....

Let's solve problems

This chart shows the number of times each Euro lottery number has been drawn over 7 years.

You need
graph paper

Ball no.	Main draw	Ball no.	Main draw	Ball no.	Main draw	Ball no.	Main draw	Ball no.	Main draw
1	78	11	83	21	61	31	88	41	63
2	84	12	80	22	68	32	78	42	63
3	77	13	56	23	87	33	78	43	84
4	71	14	81	24	72	34	63	44	88
5	70	15	71	25	88	35	78	45	79
6	72	16	66	26	71	36	74	46	77
7	75	17	72	27	83	37	65	47	85
8	69	18	72	28	83	38	104	48	74
9	79	19	65	29	71	39	66	49	73
10	74	20	57	30	75	40	86	50	72

1 Group the data for the main draw and record it in the table. Then draw a bar chart of the results.

Ball numbers	Frequency
1–10	
11–20	
21–30	
31–40	
41–50	

2 Write three things to describe what the bar chart shows or does not show.

- ______________________________
- ______________________________
- ______________________________

Using pie charts (2)

Name ....

Let's practise

You need
coloured pencils

1 Colour the fractions of each circle.

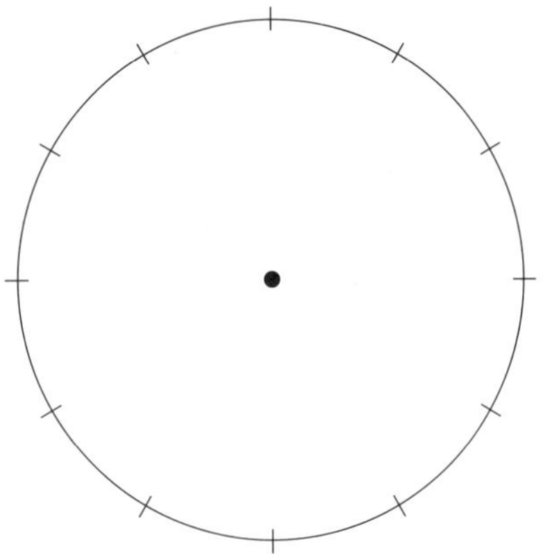

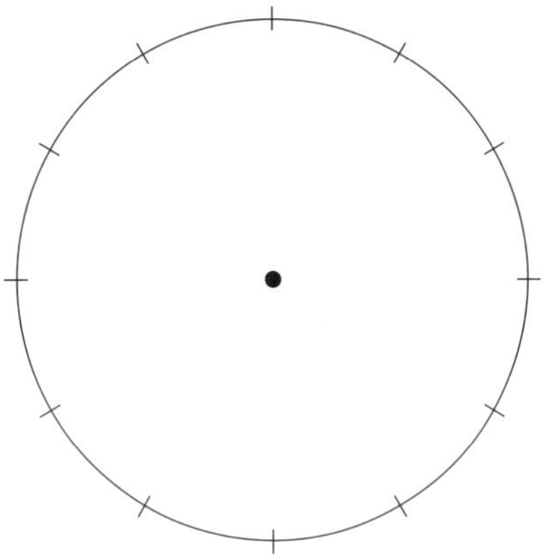

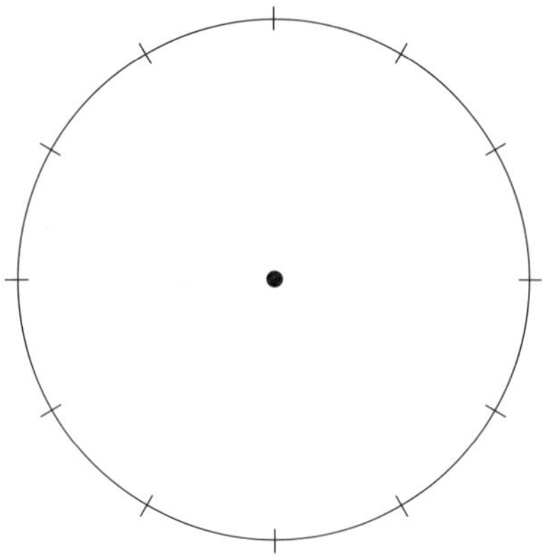

a $\frac{1}{4}$ red, $\frac{1}{2}$ blue

b $\frac{3}{4}$ red, $\frac{1}{6}$ blue

c $\frac{3}{4}$ red, $\frac{1}{12}$ blue

Let's solve problems

2 120 children hit a ball up into the air off a tennis racket as many times as they can before it hits the ground. Here are their results. Complete the pie chart to show the results.

Number of hits	Number of children
0–10	5
11–20	10
21–30	40
31–40	35
41–50	15
51–60	0
61–70	10
71–80	5

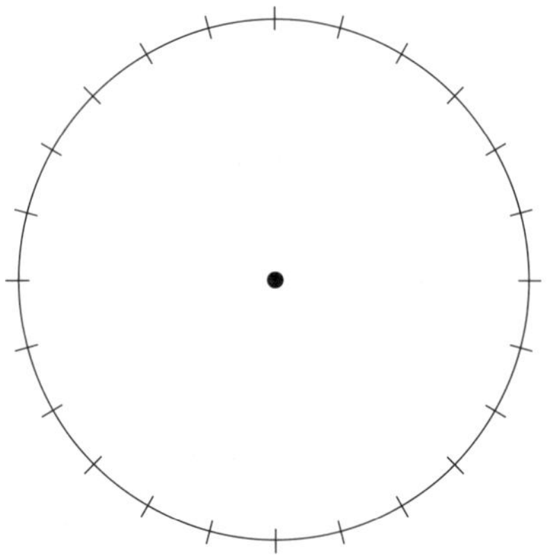

Let's investigate

You need
a protractor, reading books

3 Find 18 different books with a maximum of 200 pages.
How many pages in each book?
Use this information to make a table and a pie chart.
Remember to group the data.

Interpreting data and finding the mode and range (2)

Activity Sheet 59

Name ....

Let's investigate

Work with a partner.

You need
squared paper, a ruler

1 Here are the results of the men's 100 metres event in a world athletics championship, measured in seconds.

Final	(USA) 9·87; (Tri) 9·94; (Bar) 10·04; (GBR) 10·08; (USA) 10·09; (GBR) 10·13; (RSA) 10·17; (Gha) 10·25
Semi-finals Heat 1	(GBR) 10·13; (Bar) 10·16; (GBR) 10·16; (RSA) 10·20; (Gha) 10·26; (USA) 10·27; (Fra) 10·32; (Jam) 10·33
Semi-finals Heat 2	(USA) 10·04; (USA) 10·09; (Tri) 10·13; (Gha) 10·16; (Aus) 10·26; (Ngr) 10·32; (Ngr) 10·33; (Can) 10·34
Round 1 Heat 1	(GBR) 9·99; (USA) 10·03; (Ngr) 10·03; (Fra) 10·03; (Aus) 10·20; (Bar) 10·26; (Aus) 10·32, (Ita) 10·32
Round 1 Heat 2	(GBR) 10·12; (USA) 10·16; (Bar) 10·26; (Can) 10·26; (Fra) 10·27; (Ita) 10·27; (RSA) 10·27; (Jam) 10·30
Round 1 Heat 3	(Bar) 10·04; (Aus) 10·13; (Gha) 10·20; (Jam) 10·26; (USA) 10·26; (Fra) 10·32; (Tri) 10·32; (Can) 10·32

Aus	Australia	Fra	France	Ita	Italy	RSA	South Africa
Bar	Barbados	GBR	Great Britain	Jam	Jamaica	TRI	Trinidad
Can	Canada	Gha	Ghana	Ngr	Nigeria	USA	America

a For each heat in round 1, find the range of the times and which time is the mode. Complete the table.

	Range	**Mode**
Round 1 Heat 1		
Round 1 Heat 2		
Round 1 Heat 3		

b What is the range of the times in the whole competition? ____________________

2 **a** Group the data for the whole competition and organise it in a frequency table.

b Record the data on a bar line graph.

Time (in seconds)	**Frequency**
9·85 – 9·89	
9·90 – 9·94	
9·95 – 9·99	
10·30 – 10·34	

Finding the mean

Activity Sheet 60

Name ....

Let's practise

1 Work out whether each circled number is the mean of the set of numbers.
The first two have been done for you.

3 14 (15) 17 26
3 + 14 + 15 + 17 + 26 = 75
75 ÷ 5 = 15
YES

1 2 (5) 6 7 8
1 + 2 + 5 + 6 + 7 + 8 = 29
29 ÷ 6 = $4\frac{5}{6}$
NO

a 5 (12) 13 18

b 2 7 13 (24) 74

c 11 16 (25) 29 32

d 54 54 (120) 148 200

e 40 50 (58) 60 70

f 28 28 (34) 35 46 47

Let's investigate

2 Investigate making different sets of numbers each with a mean of 20.
Some sets may have more numbers than others.

? What if the mean was 1?